YOU BAKE 'EM
DOG BISCUITS
Cookbook

by Janine Adams

Running Press
PHILADELPHIA · LONDON

Printed in the United States

11 12 13 14 15

Digit on the right indicates the number of this printing

Library of Congress Control Number: 2004116801

ISBN-13: 978-0-7624-2336-1
ISBN-10: 0-7624-2336-6

Book design and collage illustrations by Corinda Cook
Edited by Sarah O'Brien and Diana von Glahn

Typography: Caslon, Clarendon, Script, Trade Gothic, Bodega, and Willow

This book may be ordered by mail from the publisher. Please include $2.50 for postage and handling.
But try your bookstore first!

Running Press Book Publishers
2300 Chestnut Street Suite 200
Philadelphia, PA 19103-4371

Visit us on the web!
www.runningpress.com

Acknowledgments

I am indebted to the many people who helped with this book. Above all, I want to thank my husband, Barry Marcus, a pastry chef-instructor at the Institute of Culinary Education in New York City, for his invaluable help. In addition to supplying expertise, he also displayed amazing tolerance as the house was filled daily with the aroma of liver, fish, peanut butter, or other savory smells.

In addition, I'd like to thank the wonderful recipe testers who played such a huge role in making the book possible. At the top of the list is Amy Heggie, who tested more than a dozen recipes for me, each time offering absolutely wonderful feedback. Her taste testers included her dogs Archie, Jack, Levi, and Truman, along with the visiting Maisy and various and sundry canine friends.

I am also indebted to the other recipe and taste testers: Sydney Armstrong with Miss Millie, Sadie Mae, Sassy, Snickers, and Sprite; Penny Bolton with Daisy Mae and Sherman; Sally Brown with Otis and Queenie; Robin Clark with Daisy, Morley, and Norton; Mary Lynn D'Aubin with Ike and Babs; Ann Daugherty with Gracie, Monty, Pogo, and Webster; Diane Eskenasy with Buddy, Cooper, and Cory; Erica Galipeau with Buddy; Phyllis Gerstenfeld with Billie; Denise Gwinn with Boo, Dani, and Ellis; Janyne Kizer with Emma and Hannah; Dot Kurz with Lacy; Marilyn McClaskey with Emma and Medora; Susan McCullough with Allie; Deirdre McKibbin-Vaughan with Maddie; Nisha Naik with Journey and Truman; Vicki Palmer with Xena; Susan Taylor with Lisa; Shannon Wilkinson with Booker and Tyler; Jay Wooten with Bertie, Patch, and Bingo Little.

Thank you one and all!

Contents

CHAPTER FOUR
Special Treats for Special Occasions . . . 48

CHAPTER FIVE:
Kids and Dogs: Keeping Them Happy and Safe . . . 62

CHAPTER ONE

INTRODUCTION

People seem surprised—and impressed—when I mention that I make homemade treats for my dogs. It's as if baking something for your dog is a huge extravagance, or a lot of work, when it is actually easy and inexpensive. Sometimes people will say, "I don't even bake for my family, I can't make treats for my dog!" However, these same people enjoy giving treats to their dogs. What they don't realize is that by purchasing ready-made treats, they're spending more money for what is more than likely an inferior product.

You don't have to be a Martha Stewart wannabe to enjoy baking for your dog. Take it from me. I make exactly three dishes for humans. (Luckily, I'm married to someone who cooks well.) Yet, I make all kinds of treats for my dogs.

For me, cooking for humans is a little intimidating. If I'm not precise in the measurements, the food might not taste just right. That's what makes baking for dogs so great. They don't care much about seasoning, and the appearance of the treat is more or less meaningless for them. More

likely than not, your dog will enjoy any treat you make, as long as you take into account his or her particular likes and dislikes.

My young standard poodle, Kirby, is the type of dog who will eat almost anything. Still, he does have some food preferences. From his very first sniff of it, he's hated peanut butter—won't touch the stuff or anything made with it. He doesn't care that most dogs love peanut butter. So I don't bother offering him peanut-butter-based treats.

However, Kirby will lick a cut lemon if you offer it to him. Most dogs wouldn't like lemons, so there aren't any lemon-flavored treats in this cookbook. However, if you have a dog that loves lemon (or any other flavor) feel free to alter the recipes to feature his or her favorite ingredients!

All the recipes in this book have been taste-tested by my own standard poodles, Kirby and Pip, who are actually developing a fairly discerning palate thanks to their exposure to so many different treats. Each recipe has also been tested by at least one other baker. Virtually all of them commented on how easy the recipes were to make. One of the recipe testers commented that making these treats was easier than going to the store to buy commercial treats! All of the recipe testers used their dogs (and sometimes friends' dogs, as well) as taste testers. You can trust that the treats you bake from this cookbook are not only good for your dog, but have also received the paws up from at least a couple of other dogs.

Healthy Treats

The treats in this book aren't junk food. They're not life sustaining either, so don't plan on giving your dog anything in this book as a substitute for more nutritionally balanced food. We're talking snacks only. Still, you can feel good about giving your dog a treat you make from this cookbook. It's sort of like giving your child a piece of fruit rather than a piece of candy.

What makes a dog treat healthy? The various healthful properties of major ingredients are included in Appendix One. Basically, a healthy dog treat should be made of wholesome ingredients that are good enough for humans to eat. The snack shouldn't be loaded with sugar or excess fat. Also, unlike many commercial treats, your

homemade healthy treat won't have artificial preservatives, dyes, or chemicals added. You'll know what each and every ingredient is (no more treats containing the generic "meat" or "animal digest" like some treats). If the ingredients in the recipes seem a little hard to find, consult Appendix Two for some suggested places to shop.

Some dogs have special dietary needs due to food allergies or health conditions. The chapters on treats for special dietary needs offer recipes to suit these needs. Remember that you can adapt any of the recipes to fit your dog's needs. To make a recipe low in fat, for instance, substitute applesauce for oil. If your dog has a sensitivity to chicken, substitute beef or another protein in a recipe. You get the idea. The recipes are endlessly adaptable and your effort is a very low-risk proposition since your dog is bound to be grateful.

The Well-Stocked Pantry

If you keep a few things in your pantry or freezer, you'll be able to make some treats on a whim, without a trip to the grocery store. Perhaps you'll want to reward your dog for being especially good at the dog park or for coming back to you instead of chasing that squirrel on your walk. If you have all the ingredients on hand, you can make your house smell delicious (to your dog anyway) and whip up a special treat in no time.

Staples to keep around for quick treat making include:

For your pantry:

Whole-wheat flour

Wheat germ or wheat bran

Non-grain flours (if grains cause your dog to itch)

Chicken broth

Natural peanut butter

Canned salmon

Meat baby food

Non-fat dry milk

Garlic powder

For your refrigerator and/or freezer:

Beef or chicken liver

Cheddar cheese

Parmesan cheese

Pre-chopped garlic

Milk

Short Cuts Are Good!

There are a few non-food items that you can keep on hand that will help make baking treats hassle-free. Honestly, they make things so easy that I probably wouldn't bake without them. They include:

Disposable latex gloves: These are probably my favorite treat-making accessories since I don't like getting my hands dirty. (You'd never catch me doing yard work without gardening gloves.) When I wear latex gloves in the kitchen, and I'm talking about the kind medical professionals wear, I feel invincible. I can handle raw liver with impunity and use my hands to mix batters that contain fish. I never have to worry about my hands stinking for the rest of the day. I can also touch treats to cut them before they're completely cooled. You can buy them in bulk at a warehouse discount store.

Aluminum foil or non-stick foil: I hate washing dishes. If I line a baking sheet with aluminum foil, all I have to do when I'm finished is rinse the crumbs off my baking sheet. No cooked-on anything to clean up. If I use plain foil, which is admittedly less expensive than non-stick foil, I spray it with canola oil spray. If I use non-stick foil, I don't even have to do that. The treats just slide right off. It's miraculous stuff. Some people dislike baking on foil for fear it's not healthy. If you have these concerns, just substitute baking parchment. You can also use a bare pan, greased as necessary, if you don't mind the clean up.

A food processor: You'll see that many of the recipes call for the use of a food processor. It's great for grinding up liver, for example, or for emulsifying peanut butter with milk (something that's surprisingly hard to do by hand). You could use a blender, but clean up tends to be more difficult. If you don't have a food processor, you can use a knife for chopping and a spoon for mixing, but it's a lot more work. A dishwasher-safe food processor really makes treat-making a non-chore.

A non-stick rolling pin: Some dog-treat dough can be pretty sticky. Since you don't want dog-treat ingredients coming anywhere near your next piecrust, consider buying a non-stick rolling pin that you can reserve for baking treats. Dough rarely sticks to these rolling pins, and they are easier to clean than their wooden counterparts.

Cutting mats: Thin, dishwasher-safe cutting mats make good surfaces on which to roll out dough. They're easy to clean and won't leave a mess on your counter. (An alternative is to roll the dough out onto a sheet of non-stick foil.)

Pre-shredded or pre-grated cheese:

Cheddar or Parmesan cheese can make great additions to treat recipes. Most dogs love the taste of cheese. Because shredding and grating can be labor intensive, I buy pre-shredded cheese. This makes it easy to whip up a cheese-based or cheese-enhanced recipe. Pre-crumbled blue cheese is another option.

Some Tips On Clean Up

Whenever you're working with pureed liver, you have a mess on your hands. The stuff is very sticky. Add flour to it, and it becomes a nasty paste. That's why most of the liver recipes call for you to puree the liver, before adding it to the flour in the bowl, rather than mixing the flour with the liver in the food processor. It is really challenging

to clean a nook-and-cranny-laden food processor after it has contained flour and liver.

Another important consideration when you're working with liver is to wash, or at least rinse, the food processor bowl, blade, and lid as soon as you're through with it. Once they've dried, dog-treat ingredients tend to stick. I rinse the food processor parts in soapy water, then put them in the dishwasher for a thorough washing. You'll be sorry if you let a liver-encrusted food processor sit around too long.

Storage

We're accustomed to buying dog biscuits that can sit out at room temperature without going stale or moldy. That's possible for two reasons: commercial treats tend to contain preservatives, and they're also very dry. Homemade treats are another story.

A good rule of thumb for storing the treats you make from this cookbook is to refrigerate them. Biscuits that have been dried out in the oven until virtually no moisture is left can stay out at room temperature. Treats that are moist or that contain liver or fish belong in the refrigerator. Even refrigerated, they'll mold after a while.

When I make a batch of treats, I divide the finished product into quarters. I'll fill four plastic bags with the treats, label them, and put three in the freezer. The fourth goes into the refrigerator for immediate use. I try to keep no more than a week's supply in the refrigerator. With two dogs that are amply rewarded on a daily basis, we easily go through a quarter of a recipe (or sometimes more) in a week.

The Ick Factor

A few of the treats in this book will make your house smell great (like the Pumpkin Pie Biscuits in Chapter Four). Depending on your own personal tastes, some of the treats might make you want to open all the windows while they are baking.

Liver is a common ingredient in these treats. The first time I baked liver treats, six or seven years ago, the smell made me sick. I couldn't believe how awful it was. Of course, my dogs begged to differ. They showed such great enthusiasm for the liver treats that I kept baking them. Soon, I didn't even mind the smell. Honestly. I don't think twice about baking liver treats now.

The smell of liver is one thing to get past. The way it looks and feels is another. This is where latex gloves come in. Liver is a lot easier to handle when you're wearing gloves and can't feel its slimy texture. Chicken livers, and sometimes beef liver, tend to come packaged in little one-pound tubs. For most of the liver recipes, you can just dump the contents into the food processor for pureeing—you don't even have to touch it. Of course you can still smell it. While raw liver isn't as potent a smell as cooked liver, it's still noticeable. Again, you'll get used to it.

My husband, Barry, who has the nose of a bloodhound, actually thinks that the smell of cooking fish treats is worse than liver. In his opinion, the worst smell of all is peanut butter treats. To each his (or her) own!

Yields

I purposely didn't list yields on these recipes because the size of the treat is completely dependent upon the size of the dog that will be eating it. Obviously, the smaller each treat, the more you'll get out of a recipe. With the exception of the frozen treats in Chapter Five, the recipes generally start out with the same amount of raw ingredients and make roughly the same yield.

CHAPTER TWO

Good Dog Biscuits

Biscuits are the classic dog treat. If you had a dog when you were a kid, you probably fed him or her a hard, bone-shaped treat. I'd be willing to bet it was a Milk-bone® brand dog biscuit. Biscuits are a wonderful way to reward your dog. Dogs love chewing them up, and you feel good about giving your dog a treat.

Homemade dog biscuits don't have to be bone shaped, though they certainly can be. You can use cookie cutters in any shape to make your biscuits. Around here, most biscuits are made with a star-shaped cookie cutter or a heart-shaped one. (It might sound silly, but it feels like I'm saying "I love you" when I give my dog a heart-shaped biscuit.) A kitchen supply store will have a number of shapes from which you can choose. When selecting cookie cutters for making dog biscuits, bear the following in mind:

• **Size:** The biscuit made with the cutter should not be too big for your dog to eat easily. Select a cutter appropriate for the size of your dog.

• **Shape:** Don't pick a cutter that has a lot of angles, especially onc with any small sections. They can be hard to get out of the cutter and on to the baking sheet in one piece or without losing shape. I have a poodle-shaped cookie cutter, for instance, that's hard to use. The resulting biscuits barely resemble a poodle.

• **Ease of cleaning:** The ideal cookie cutter can be washed in the dishwasher. Since dog-biscuit dough is sometimes sticky, cookie cutters can be a little tedious to clean by hand.

Soft Versus Crunchy

Traditionally, dog biscuits are hard and crunchy. Some people think that the crunchiness cleans the dog's teeth, though many experts cast doubt on this belief. In any case, feeding a dog hard biscuits isn't a substitute for brushing your dog's teeth or for giving him or her actual raw bones to chew on.

Whether you choose to make hard biscuits

or soft ones is a matter of personal preference for both you and your dog. Crunchier biscuits tend to take longer to eat, which might maximize the chewing pleasure for your dog. They also take longer to bake since you typically leave them in a low oven for a long time to dry out.

Some dogs—including mine—seem to prefer a softer treat that they can swallow after a few chomps. I think it's the flavor of the treat, not the actual eating, that they enjoy. It may seem crazy, but sometimes I just don't want to make my dogs work that hard to eat a treat!

If your dog prefers hard biscuits, turn down the oven to 200° F or lower after the initial baking time and continue cooking until they are the desired hardness. If you are baking at night, you can turn off the oven and leave the pan in to cool overnight.

Other Types Of Cookies

Most of the recipes in this chapter are for biscuits you cut out with cookie cutters. There are also some recipes for drop cookies. These are quicker and a little less messy to prepare. Dough made with meat, like liver or ground turkey, tends to be sticky. This type of dough lends itself more easily to drop cookies. These treats look a little unconventional, but your dog won't care!

One thing to bear in mind when making drop cookies is to make them bite sized. Depending on the size of your dog, these are going to be much smaller than the cookies you'd make for yourself. If a drop cookie is so large that it requires a few bites, it will leave crumbs. If your dog won't suck up all the crumbs, you'll be stuck vacuuming or sweeping.

Biscuits As Gifts

Dog biscuits make terrific gifts for dog lovers. One Christmas, I gave all my friends' dogs homemade biscuits in lieu of gifts for the friends themselves. The gifts were a big hit with both dogs and humans.

Part of the fun is packaging them for gift giving. I used gift boxes in the shape of Chinese food take-out containers. I lined them with waxed paper to avoid any oil soaking through. Since then, I've found some great gift-box Chinese food containers designed especially for dog gifts, with paw prints or bones printed on them. They're wax-lined, so you don't have to worry about oil seepage. They're available at a great website called

Doggone Good (www.doggonegood.com). As I write this book, they cost $0.95 to $2.25 each, and even less if purchased in bulk. Given how inexpensive ingredients for dog treats can be, you can give a beautifully packaged, delicious gift for very little expense.

In addition to the Chinese food containers, there are other imaginative ways to package biscuits. Here are just a few ideas:

• **Decorative gift bags lined with matching tissue paper.** Wrap your treats in colorful plastic wrap and wrap a ribbon around each bundle.

• **Disposable storage containers.** These are great for storage and gift giving. You can wrap them in wrapping paper, stack them and tie them with a ribbon, or decorate the lid. At holiday time, these containers come in holiday colors.

• **Cookie tins.** Put dog biscuits in a holiday tin, just like you might do with holiday cookies intended for human consumption. The tin itself becomes a nice gift that can be reused (perhaps as a gift for someone else).

• **Gift tags stamped with dog-themed rubber stamps.** There are many dog-themed rubber stamps available at specialty stores. Simply pick up some blank manila tie-on tags at an office-supply store and you have a great canvas for making dog-themed gift tags.

Consider giving a copy of
this book with your gift of dog biscuits.
The treats are a gift for the dog,
but the book is something the human
can use for years to come!

Easy Cream Cheese Biscuits

I've never met a dog who didn't like cream cheese. This biscuit has all the flavor of cream cheese, plus garlic and milk. It's very easy to make because you basically dump all the ingredients in the food processor and mix to form a dough ball.

1 package ($^1/_4$ ounce) dry yeast

$^1/_4$ cup warm water

$2^1/_3$ cups whole-wheat flour, plus extra for rolling

$^1/_4$ cup unsweetened applesauce

4 ounces cream cheese

1 egg

$^1/_4$ cup powdered milk, plus extra for rolling

1 teaspoon garlic powder

- Preheat the oven to 350° F.
- In a small bowl, dissolve the yeast in the warm water. Combine with all ingredients in a food processor and mix into dough (or mix by hand in a bowl). Roll out on a floured surface to $^1/_4$-inch thickness. Sprinkle the dough with extra dry milk to make it easier to roll out. Cut into shapes with your favorite cookie cutters. Place biscuits on a cookie sheet covered with greased or non-stick foil. Bake for 20 to 25 minutes or until a light, golden brown. Store in an airtight container in the refrigerator.

Sweet and Savory Biscuits

This recipe is a good example of how easy it is to make substitutions in dog treat recipes. It calls for black-strap molasses, which is higher in minerals and generally more nutritious (though less sweet) than regular molasses. You can substitute regular molasses or honey, if you prefer. Similarly, any type of plant-based oil will work if you don't have safflower oil handy. You can also substitute half a pound (about $^3/_4$ cup) of Simple Liver Puree (see page 112) for the baby food in this recipe.

$2^1/_4$ cups whole wheat flour, plus extra for rolling

1 cup barley flour

$^1/_2$ cup wheat bran

$^1/_2$ teaspoon salt

1 tablespoon blackstrap molasses

1 egg

1 cup yogurt

1 tablespoon safflower oil

3 (2.5-ounce) jars of meat-only baby food

- Preheat the oven to 325° F.
- In a large bowl, combine the flours, bran and salt. In a food processor, combine the molasses, egg, yogurt, oil, and baby food. Puree it into a liquid and add to the dry mixture. Stir with a spoon, then knead with your hands to incorporate all the flour. Turn out on to a floured surface. Sprinkle more flour on top of the dough and roll to a $^1/_2$-inch thickness. Cut into desired shape with cookie cutters. Place biscuits on a baking sheet covered with greased or non-stick foil. Bake for 25 minutes or until browned. Store in an airtight container in the refrigerator.

Bacon-Cheese Biscuits

Dogs (like most people) love bacon. These biscuits provide lots of bacon flavor (and smell) without adding too much fat.

1 cup whole wheat flour, plus $^1/_4$ cup as needed and a little extra for rolling

1 cup soy flour

$^1/_2$ cup wheat bran

$^1/_2$ cup grated Parmesan cheese

$^1/_4$ cup unsweetened applesauce

$^3/_4$ cup water

1 egg

$^1/_4$ cup (about six slices) cooked, drained, crumbled bacon

- Preheat the oven to 350° F.

- In a large bowl, combine the flours, wheat bran, and cheese. Add the applesauce, water, egg, and bacon. Stir into a dough. If the dough is very sticky, knead in an additional $^1/_4$ cup of flour.

- Turn the dough out onto a floured surface and, with a floured (or non-stick) rolling pin, roll to $^1/_4$-inch thickness. Cut into shapes with cookie cutters. Place biscuits on a baking sheet and bake for 20 minutes or until brown. Store in an airtight container in the refrigerator.

Peanut Butter Oat Biscuits

Most dogs love the flavor of peanut butter. If you use health-food-store peanut butter, that's basically nothing but ground peanuts (you can grind it fresh yourself at some stores), it makes a healthy flavoring for treats.

2 cups all-purpose flour

$1/2$ cup wheat germ

$1/2$ cup oat bran

1 cup milk

$1/2$ cup natural peanut butter

1 egg

- Preheat the oven to 350° F.
- In a large bowl, combine the dry ingredients. In the food processor, combine the milk and peanut butter and process to liquefy. Add the egg and process until egg is mixed in. Pour the liquid mixture into the dry mixture and stir into dough. Turn dough out onto a lightly floured surface and roll to $1/4$-inch thickness. Use cookie cutters to cut into shapes. Place biscuits on a baking sheet covered with greased or non-stick foil. Bake for 30 minutes or until lightly browned on top. Store in the refrigerator in an airtight container.

Fruity Biscuits

The berries used in this recipe make the biscuits an unusual purplish color. If you use raspberries only, they'll be pink, which can make a fun Valentine's Day or Christmas biscuit. If you don't have blueberries or raspberries on hand, you can try some other type of fruit. This biscuit's sweetness is a real treat for dogs with a sweet tooth.

For the egg wash:

1 egg

Pinch of salt

For the batter:

1 cup whole wheat flour, plus extra for rolling	**$\frac{1}{4}$ cup blueberries (fresh or frozen)**
1 cup all-purpose flour	**$\frac{1}{2}$ cup raspberries (fresh or frozen)**
1 cup soy flour	**2 tablespoons honey**
2 tablespoons flax seed meal or wheat germ	**1 tablespoon safflower oil**
$\frac{1}{2}$ teaspoon ground cinnamon	**2 eggs**
$\frac{1}{2}$ cup warm water	**1 teaspoon vanilla**

- Preheat the oven to 375° F.

- For the egg wash, beat one egg in a small bowl and add a pinch of salt. Set aside.

- In a large bowl, combine the flours, flax seed meal or wheat germ, and cinnamon. In a food processor, combine the water, fruit, honey, oil, the two eggs, and vanilla. Pulse until smooth. Pour the liquid ingredients over the dry ingredients and stir to combine. (Don't fret if there are little pieces of fruit visible.) Knead the dough in the bowl until it makes a nice ball and turn it out onto a lightly floured surface. Roll out to $\frac{1}{4}$-inch thickness and cut with cookie cutters. Place biscuits on ungreased baking sheets. Using a pastry brush, brush egg wash on top of each biscuit. Bake for 15 minutes or until the tops are browned. For crunchier cookies, turn the oven down to 200° F and bake for an additional hour or two, or until they reach the desired crunchiness. Store at room temperature in a loosely covered container.

Cheddar Biscuits

Dogs love cheese! Any type of cheese will do for this recipe, so if you don't have cheddar on hand, try mozzarella, Swiss, or any other cheese you have in the refrigerator.

1 cup all-purpose flour

1 cup whole wheat flour

1 cup shredded cheddar cheese

2 tablespoons butter

3/4 cup milk

Grated Parmesan cheese for topping

- Preheat the oven to 375° F.

- Put flours and cheese into food processor. Pulse to mix. Add butter and milk. Mix well. Turn out onto a floured surface and roll out to 1/4- to 1/2-inch thickness. Poke with tines of fork and sprinkle with grated Parmesan cheese. Cut into shapes with cookie cutters. Place on baking sheet covered with greased or non-stick foil. Bake for 15 to 20 minutes or until golden brown. Store in an airtight container in the refrigerator.

Chicken Liver Biscuits

Biscuit dough made with liver can be sticky, which can make it difficult to roll out. If this occurs, knead a little flour into the dough. Also, liberally sprinkle the rolling surface and rolling pin with flour. Your dog will think it's worth the effort!

1 cup whole wheat flour

1 cup soy flour

1 cup wheat germ

$1/2$ teaspoon salt

$1/2$ pound (1 cup) chicken livers

2 tablespoons olive oil

2 eggs

$1/4$ cup water reserved from cooking livers

- Preheat the oven to 400° F.
- Combine flours, wheat germ, and salt in a large bowl. Set aside. Place the chicken livers in a saucepan and cover with water. Bring to a boil and simmer until cooked—2 to 3 minutes. Drain the livers, retaining $1/4$ cup of the cooking liquid.
- In a food processor, mix the cooked livers, oil, eggs, and liver water until well blended. Add to the dry mixture, stirring with a spoon and then kneading with your hands. Turn out onto a lightly floured surface, and roll to $1/2$-inch thick. (Sprinkle flour on top of the dough if it's sticky.) Use cookie cutters to cut into shapes and place on a baking sheet. Bake for 15 minutes or until firm. Bottoms should be slightly browned. Store in an airtight container in the refrigerator.

Sesame Peanut Butter Biscuits

This treat is light on peanut butter. You can add more (though you may have to add a little more milk and perhaps some flour) for a more intense peanut flavor. The sesame seeds give the treat a fancy look—quite suitable for gift giving.

For the topping:

1 egg, beaten with a pinch of salt

1 tablespoon sesame seeds

For the batter:

2^1/$_4$ cups whole wheat flour, plus extra for rolling

^{3}/$_4$ cup wheat bran

^{1}/$_4$ cup natural peanut butter

^{1}/$_4$ cup milk

^{1}/$_2$ cup unsweetened applesauce

2 eggs

• Preheat the oven to 350° F.

• Beat the egg with a pinch of salt and set aside.

• Mix the flour and wheat bran together in a large bowl. In the food processor, mix the peanut butter and milk, until the peanut butter is liquefied. Add the applesauce and the two eggs and mix well. Add the liquid mixture to the dry mixture and stir into a stiff dough. Turn the dough out onto a lightly floured surface. Roll to ^{1}/$_4$- to ^{1}/$_2$-inch thickness. Use cookie cutters to cut into shapes. Place biscuits on a baking sheet. Brush each cookie with beaten egg and sprinkle with sesame seeds. Bake for 25 to 30 minutes or until the tops and bottoms brown. Store at room temperature in a loosely covered container.

Garlic Crisps

These crispy treats are easy to make. They have a strong garlic smell and flavor, which most dogs go crazy over! Make them whatever size works best for you—larger for a biscuit-like snack, or tiny for use in training sessions.

$1^1/_2$ cups whole wheat flour

4 to 6 cloves of garlic (or 1 tablespoon of pre-chopped garlic)

$^1/_4$ cup water

2 tablespoons of sunflower seeds or walnuts

2 tablespoons safflower oil

1 egg

$^1/_4$ cup grated Parmesan cheese

Garlic powder (optional)

• Preheat the oven to 400° F.

• Put all the ingredients in the food processor and mix to form a dough ball. Turn the dough out onto a lightly floured surface. Knead in some flour if the dough is too sticky to easily roll out. Roll quite thin—$^1/_8$- to $^1/_4$-inch thickness. Sprinkle with garlic powder, if desired. Place the rolled-out dough on a baking sheet covered with greased or non-stick foil. With a pizza cutter or knife, cut the dough into squares as large or small as you want, depending on the size of your dog. Prick each square with a fork, pressing hard enough for the tines to penetrate all the way through the dough.

• Bake for about 30 minutes or until the tops are brown. If you like, turn off the oven and let the crackers cool inside so they'll be even crispier. Store at room temperature in a loosely covered container.

Applesauce Cheddar Drop Cookies

Drop cookies are easy to make since you don't have to roll out dough and cut out cookies. Unless your dog is very large, you'll want to make these smaller than you would make cookies for yourself, to avoid a mess when your dog is eating them.

1 cup all-purpose flour

1 cup whole wheat flour

$^1/_2$ cup oat bran

$^1/_2$ teaspoon baking soda

$^1/_2$ teaspoon salt

$^1/_2$ teaspoon ground cinnamon

$^3/_4$ cup applesauce

$^1/_4$ cup honey

2 eggs, beaten

1 teaspoon vanilla extract

$^1/_4$ cup walnut chips (or chopped walnuts)

1 cup shredded cheddar cheese

- Preheat the oven to 375° F.

- In a large bowl, mix together the dry ingredients. Add the applesauce, honey, eggs, vanilla, and walnuts and stir together with a spoon. Fold in the cheese. Drop in small rounded teaspoonfuls (or the most appropriate size for your dog) onto a baking sheet covered in foil. Bake for 15 minutes or until the tops and bottoms are brown. Store in an airtight container in the refrigerator.

Turkey Drop Cookies

These cookies are quite soft, making them easy for aged dogs to eat. They won't flatten while baking, so if you like a flat cookie, press them down before you put them in the oven.

1 package (¹/₄ ounce) dry yeast

¹/₄ cup warm (not hot) water

1 teaspoon molasses

1 cup whole wheat flour

1¹/₂ cups all-purpose flour

1 package (¹/₄ ounce) unflavored gelatin

1 cup non-fat dry milk

8 ounces (1 cup) raw ground turkey

¹/₄ cup oil

1 egg

¹/₄ cup water at room temperature

- Preheat the oven to 300° F.

- In a medium bowl, dissolve the yeast in the warm water and add the molasses. Let sit for 10 minutes. If the yeast is active, it should double in volume. (If it doesn't, try a fresh packet of yeast.)

- Meanwhile, in a large bowl, mix together the flours, gelatin, and dried milk. Break up the raw ground turkey with your fingers as you add it to the dry mixture and stir until the turkey is fairly evenly distributed. Add the remaining wet ingredients and yeast mixture and mix it all together. Knead in the bowl to incorporate all the flour.

- Form the dough into small balls and place on a baking sheet covered with greased or non-stick foil. (A melon baller works nicely for this task.) Bake for 25 to 30 minutes or until cookies are firm. Store in an airtight container in the refrigerator.

Liver and Oat Cookies

These drop cookies retain their shape. They can be left soft (especially good for older dogs who may not have as many teeth) or made harder by leaving them in the oven longer.

$1^1/_4$ **cup quick oats**

$^1/_4$ **cup non-fat dry milk**

$^1/_4$ **cup wheat germ**

$^1/_4$ **pound ($^1/_2$ cup) beef or chicken liver**

1 egg

$^1/_4$ **cup safflower oil**

- Preheat the oven to 350° F.
- Combine dry ingredients in a large bowl. Puree liver in a food processor, then add the egg and oil. Mix together. Add this wet mixture to the dry ingredients. Mix with a spoon to cookie-dough consistency. With a teaspoon, drop batter 1 inch apart onto a baking sheet covered with greased or non-stick foil. Bake at 350° F for 15 to 20 minutes or until cookies are firm to the touch. Turn off oven. For harder consistency, leave cookies inside cooling oven for 1 to 2 hours or overnight. Store in an airtight container in the refrigerator.

CHAPTER THREE

Training Treats

Most trainers recommend using food in training. Rewarding your dog for doing what you ask, rather than correcting him for misbehavior, is not only effective, it keeps training sessions fun for your dog. It's also a lot more enjoyable (for both you and your dog) than training with corrections.

If you feel that your dog isn't motivated by food, think again. You probably just haven't tried the right food. Many beginning trainers use pieces of the dog's kibble or plain Cheerios as a reward. Some dogs, however, simply don't find those rewards worth the effort. If you whip up some of the training treats from the recipes in this chapter, you'll doubtless find a treat for which your dog is more than willing to work. Then the fun training can really begin.

What Makes a Good Training Treat?

Since you don't want your dog to fill up on treats too quickly during a training session (nor do you want to make him or her fat), it's important to use small treats when training. By small, I mean *tiny*. The best training treats are soft and not too chewy, so your dog can ingest them quickly and move on to the next activity. Pieces of hard biscuit aren't ideal—they are too crunchy. They're also hard to subdivide into smaller pieces on the fly.

The treats in this chapter can all be cut into bite-size pieces. You'll be able to make them even smaller while you're using them, simply by pinching off smaller pieces.

Training treats shouldn't be too rich or they might cause diarrhea. If you find that your dog gets diarrhea after a training session, make the treats smaller or change the main ingredient of the treat. Liver, for example, can give some dogs loose stools. If your dog flips for liver, try reducing the proportion of liver in the recipe or select a less liver-intensive recipe.

Vary Your Treats

Dogs get sick of foods just like we do. To make treats more rewarding, vary them. You can do that by mixing different treats in your treat pouch, so that you randomly select what your dog's going to get, to keep him or her guessing. You can also prioritize the various treats, saving the highest-impact treats for your dog's best feats.

Another good reason to keep a mix of treats on hand is that your dog might develop sensitivity to one or more of the ingredients in a frequently used recipe. When you're training your dog, you can go through an immense number of treats. As I write this book, Kirby is between six months and a year old—prime time for learning new things and for developing naughty habits. We're using lots of treats, particularly on our walks, to help teach him how to behave politely. If I used only one type of treat, I might ruin that treat for the years to come.

If you have time to make more than one type of recipe in a sitting, do so. Don't worry about making too many treats. Just place extra treats in a freezer bag and pop them in the freezer. They'll be ready for your next training session and you'll be glad you have them on hand.

How to Use Treats in Training

If you're interested in training your dog in a group situation, by all means enroll in a positive training class. Look for one that encourages the use of treats in training. Clicker training, which uses treats and a small plastic device that makes a "click" sound to mark the behavior you're rewarding, is especially effective, in my opinion. (See page 40) If you're trying to decide whether a particular class is truly positive, visit before enrolling. Take a look at the collars the dogs are wearing. There's no room for choke chains or prong collars in positive classes. Listen to how the humans and dogs are interacting. You should hear lots of upbeat praise and no shouting or admonishing.

Before you go to class, bake up a storm. Take along a pouch or carpenter's apron so you'll be able to get to your treats easily. Bring along more treats than you think you need so you won't run out. You'll be delighted at the ways your homemade treats will help motivate your dog to work and learn.

If you're not looking to take a class just yet (or ever), you can still incorporate training treats

into your daily routine. Every interaction with your dog is a training opportunity. Put a bunch of bite-size treats in a plastic bag in your pocket or, better yet, in a treat pouch. Take them with you when you go on walks. If your dog tends to pull, reward him or her when the leash is slack. Treats make great lures for getting your dog to move away from a distraction. If you're looking to keep your dog from raising a ruckus over another dog on your walk, try sticking a treat in his or her face while you pass the dog.

Treats are also great for creating positive associations with scary things. For instance, if your dog always barks at dogs on the other side of the street, ask for a sit and dispense treats until the dog passes. It doesn't matter if the barking persists—what you're trying to accomplish is changing how your dog feels about strange dogs. After you do this for a while, he or she will start to anticipate treats whenever a dog comes into view. Isn't that better than your dog anticipating getting yanked by the collar, yelled at, or dragged away?

The Jackpot

When you're training your dog—particularly if you're training a specific behavior—you've got a great treat-related ace in the hole. When your dog figures out what you want and performs that desired behavior, you can reward him or her with a jackpot, an extra-special treat. Reserve an especially delicious treat for this purpose or just reward your dog with a larger-than-usual portion. When your dog performs the feat, get excited and toss a whole handful of treats on the ground or feed him or her a handful, one treat at a time, until your dog thinks the supply may never stop. Trainers believe that this can make a real impact on the dog and increase the likelihood that the desired behavior will be repeated.

Special Treats for Special Feats

What is the most important thing that your dog needs to learn to do every time you ask for it? For many dog owners, it's coming when called. That's a skill that could save your dog's life. It's something you want your dog to do the first time you ask, each and every time you ask it.

The best way to teach a recall (as trainers

call coming when called) is to make coming to you the best thing your dog could want to do. That means that you should give him a treat each and every time he does it. If you really want to strengthen the behavior and make training easier and more reliable, identify a treat that your dog absolutely loves and give it to him or her only for a successful recall. If your dog is crazy about this treat and if the treat appears only after he or she hears the word "Come," your chances are greatly enhanced that your dog will drop whatever he or she is doing and come when you ask. (If your dog has a history of ignoring the word "Come," consider retraining the skill with a new word, like "Here.")

Make sure you keep it easy at first. Don't ask your dog to come while he or she is chasing a rabbit. At the beginning, call your dog between you and another person, giving a morsel of that great treat each time. Gradually increase the

distance (always working in a securely fenced area if your dog is off-leash). End each of these mini-sessions with a bang by giving a jackpot of the special treat. That way, your dog will welcome being asked to come to you the next time. Your goal is to make yourself more interesting than a squirrel or a chicken bone.

Treats Must Be Accessible

If you can't get to your training treats quickly and easily, you slow down training and risk having your dog forget what you're rewarding, even if you use a clicker. So don't keep your treats on the table or across the room. Keep them on your person. You can use a fanny pack, a carpenter's apron, or a special treat pouch (or bait bag, as they're sometimes called) made for the purpose.

If you can't envision yourself walking around the house all evening wearing a bait bag, stash treats around the house where your dog can't reach them. For example, if you're working on improving your dog's behavior at the door, keep treats near the door. Using homemade treats, however, could create a problem with this plan since many have to be refrigerated. One solution is to use dry treats (like the Grain-Free Liver Crunchies found in Chapter Seven). You can also make a point of stocking your treat spots with treats fresh from the refrigerator every morning, discarding any you didn't use the day before.

Keeping treats handy in the house allows you to reward good behavior whenever you're interacting with your dog. In life, it can be very easy to focus on undesirable behaviors and not even notice good behavior. However, if you can turn your thinking around and remember to reward your dog for doing what you what him or her to do (for example, lying quietly on a dog bed while you're watching TV), you have a much better chance of living with a hassle-free dog. Keeping treats handy makes that kind of real-life rewarding possible.

Clicker Training in a Nutshell

Clicker training—which is gaining in popularity and acceptance—is a positive training method based on the principles of operant conditioning. A clicker is a small, handheld device that clicks when you press it. The most common type of clicker is a small plastic box with a piece of metal in it that you click with your thumb. You click the clicker the moment your dog does something you want to reward. Every time you click, you give your dog a treat. Your dog quickly understands that a click means a treat is on the way. Your dog also understands that what he or she is doing when the clicker sounds is the thing that you're rewarding.

Why use a clicker when you can just reward with a treat? A click is much more precise. If you're teaching a sit, for instance, you can click the moment your dog's fanny hits the floor. If you were rewarding directly with a treat, by the time you got to your dog with the treat he or she might have already popped up again into a standing position. So your dog would have no way of knowing it was the sit that was being rewarded.

This precision allows you to mark small changes in behaviors and build on past behaviors. Clicker savvy dogs repeat behaviors they've been clicked for in the past. When you get to that point (which happens very quickly) you're on your way to shaping lots of great behaviors.

Dogs love clicker training—the sessions are fun, upbeat, and short. When you pull out the clicker, your dog will jump for joy. This method of training doesn't require corrections (if your dog does something you don't want, you just ignore it and click when he or she does the right thing). There's no yelling or hard feelings. Your dog gets paid for working. Everybody wins!

Liver Rye Training Treats

This makes a somewhat dense, cakey treat that's very easy to handle during a training session. Be sure to grind the liver well, to avoid stringy pieces that are hard to cut through. Once you think it's well combined, process it a little bit longer.

1 cup whole wheat flour

1 cup rye flour

1 pound (2 cups) beef liver (with juice)

$1/4$ cup olive oil

3 eggs

- Preheat the oven to 400° F.
- In a large bowl, combine the flours. Puree the liver in the food processor. Once liquefied, add olive oil and eggs and continue processing until well combined. Pour the liver mixture into the dry mixture and mix with a spoon into a sticky batter. Pour onto a baking sheet covered with greased or non-stick foil and spread evenly with a wet spatula or wet hands. Bake for 15 minutes or until the top is firm. Remove from the oven and cool for about a half hour or until cool enough to handle. Then turn the dough over, peel off the foil and cut into small treats. Store in an airtight container in the refrigerator.

Cheesy Salmon Training Treats

This is a soft and tasty (albeit a tad smelly) treat that your dog can gobble up quickly during a training session. You might find that the top crust puffs up a bit, which can make cutting it difficult. If that happens, just pull the top thin crust off before cutting.

---

1 (14.5-ounce) can of salmon, or 2 (7-ounce) cans

$^1/_2$ cup ricotta cheese

1 egg

$1^1/_2$ cups whole wheat flour

$^1/_4$ cup oat or wheat bran

$^1/_2$ cup shredded cheddar cheese

• Preheat the oven to 350° F.

• Empty can(s) of salmon (liquid, bones and all) into a food processor. Add ricotta and egg to the salmon and mix together well, into a mousse-like consistency. Add the flour, bran, and cheddar to the food processor and mix into a soft, sticky dough. Turn dough out onto a $13^1/_4$ x $9^1/_4$-inch baking sheet covered with greased or non-stick foil and push flat to the pan's edges with wet hands. Bake for 40 minutes or until golden brown. When cool enough to handle, turn the dough over, peel off the foil and cut into small treats. Store in an airtight container in the refrigerator.

Liver Leather

This is a terrific training treat. It's smooth, dry and just a little chewy. Best of all, it seems to appeal to even the pickiest of dogs. One of the testers described this treat as magic! This treat molds fairly quickly, so be sure to store it in the refrigerator and freeze any you can't use within a few days.

1 pound (2 cups) beef or chicken livers

1 cup tapioca flour or starch

- Preheat the oven to 250° F.
- Puree the liver in a food processor. Add the tapioca flour or starch and mix well. Line a baking sheet with foil and lightly grease it (or use non-stick foil). Pour the mixture onto the baking sheet and bake for 70 minutes or until firm on top and uniformly brown on the bottom. Place baking sheet on cooling rack and let sit until cool enough to handle. Peel off the foil and cut into small pieces with a pizza cutter. Store in an airtight container in the refrigerator.

Blue Cheese Walnut Training Treats

If your dog has an adventurous palate, he'll probably go wild for the zingy flavor of blue cheese. This recipe adds a little honey to play off the tang of the cheese. These bite-sized treats make terrific, easy-to-use training treats.

$1^1/_2$ **cups whole wheat flour**

$^1/_2$ **cup oat or wheat bran**

$^1/_2$ **teaspoon baking soda**

$^1/_4$ **cup finely chopped walnuts or pecans**

$^1/_4$ **cup safflower oil**

$^1/_4$ **cup honey**

2 eggs, beaten

1 cup blue cheese crumbles

- Preheat the oven to 350° F.

- In a large bowl, mix together the flour, bran, baking soda, and nuts. Add the oil, honey, eggs, and blue cheese and stir together with a spoon. Form into bite-sized balls and place onto a baking sheet covered with greased or non-stick foil. Bake for 10 to 15 minutes or until the tops and bottoms are brown. Store in an airtight container in the refrigerator.

Cheesy Liver Training Treats

This treat calls for pulverized freeze-dried liver. If you prefer, you can use fresh beef or chicken liver. Simply puree $^1/_4$ pound ($^1/_2$ cup) or more beef or chicken liver in the food processor and add to the dry ingredients with the milk and egg.

2 cups whole wheat flour

$^1/_2$ cup oat bran

$^1/_4$ cup freeze-dried liver powder (see below)

$^1/_4$ cup grated Parmesan cheese

1 large egg

$^3/_4$ cup milk

- Preheat the oven to 350° F.
- Mix the dry ingredients together in a large bowl. Add the egg and milk and mix into a dough. Roll out the dough to $^1/_4$-inch thickness and place on a baking sheet covered with greased or non-stick foil. Sprinkle with additional grated Parmesan. Bake for 25 to 30 minutes, or until golden brown. When cool enough to handle, turn the dough over, peel off the foil and cut into small treats. Store in an airtight container in the refrigerator or freeze any treats you won't be able to use within a week.
- To make liver powder: Pulverize freeze-dried liver treats in a food processor or blender.

Liver Jerky Bites

The key to these ugly, but tasty, jerky bites is boiling the liver before you bake it. Cut the treats to whatever size pleases you and your dog. Once cooked, they're not easy to break into smaller pieces. The liver will look shrunken and charred, but your dog won't mind!

1 pound (2 cups) (or more or less, as desired) beef or chicken liver

- Preheat the oven to 250° F.
- Cut the liver into bite-sized pieces. Place in a saucepan and cover with water. Bring water to a boil, then lower the heat and simmer for three minutes. Drain the water and place pieces of liver on a baking sheet covered with greased or non-stick foil. Bake the liver for two hours (longer if pieces are large). Store at room temperature in a loosely covered container.

Yummy Training Meatballs

This recipe makes a nice, dense meatball or meatloaf, that's very easy to break up. If you find making the meatballs tedious (as I do), you can make a meatloaf instead, and cut it into training-sized treats after it's cooled.

1 pound (2 cups) hamburger or ground turkey

1 tablespoon grated Parmesan cheese

1 teaspoon dried parsley

$^1/_2$ teaspoon dried dill

Liver bread crumbs (see recipe below)

• Preheat the oven to 350° F.

• Combine all ingredients in a large bowl and mix together with your hands. Form small, treat-sized meatballs by rolling a pinch of the meat mixture between your palms. Place on a baking sheet lined with greased or non-stick foil. Bake for 7 to 10 minutes or until browned and cooked through. Remove cooked meatballs onto paper towels to absorb excess grease.

• ***Alternative baking method:*** Rather than forming meatballs, put the whole mixture into a loaf pan. (I line the loaf pan with non-stick foil, to make clean up easier.) Bake the loaf for about 60 minutes or until dry on top. If you're using anything but the leanest meat, drain off the fat after you take it out of the oven. Once cooled, cut the meatloaf into small training bites. Store in the refrigerator in an airtight container.

For liver bread crumbs:

Place three pieces of bread and three freeze-dried liver treats in food processor. Mix until liver is completely chopped up. (Don't bother to measure the crumbs—just dump this amount in the mixing bowl.)

CHAPTER FOUR

Special Treats for Special Occasions

For many people—particularly those of us so in love with our dogs that we bake treats for them—pets are a very real part of the family. That's why so many pet owners include their pets in holiday celebrations. According to a 2003 survey by the American Animal Hospital Association, 63 percent of respondents celebrate their pet's birthday. Another 67 percent include their pets in celebration of holidays like Halloween, Thanksgiving, and Christmas.

Baking something appropriate to the occasion (like the red and green Christmas dog biscuits, pumpkin-flavored Thanksgiving cookies, or heart-shaped Valentine sandwiches) is fun way to include your dog in the holiday celebrations.

Sharing your holiday meal with your dog is a nice thing to do (providing you eat healthily), but you must be sure not to load your dog up with fatty food. Too much fat can cause acute pancreatitis, a painful inflammation of the pancreas that could land you and your dog at the emergency vet clinic. When sharing foods with your dog, avoid those that are safe for humans but toxic to dogs. These include chocolate (though carob is okay), onions, raisins, and grapes. Also, according to the ASPCA Animal Poison Control Center, products that contain the artificial sweetener Xylitol can be toxic to dogs.

Throwing a Doggy Party

Making birthdays or gotcha days (the anniversary of an adoption) extra special can be challenging. For many well-loved dogs, food, treats, and toys are so abundant that every day feels like a special occasion.

One sure-fire way to make an occasion special is to have a party. If you invite your dog's canine friends over for a birthday party, your dog is guaranteed to find the day memorable. This chapter has recipes for some special treats (like mini muffins) that are easy to serve at a party. Of course, any home-baked treat will be well received by canine party guests!

When planning a party for a dog, just like planning a party with a human guest of honor, there are a few basics you need to decide upon right away, including: venue, guests, introductions, menu, and activities.

Venue

If you live in a city, there might be a dog bakery, day care center, or training facility you can rent out for the party. Heck, they might even provide food and entertainment! You don't have to go to that expense, however. If you have a large enough home (or rumpus room) and/or a fenced back yard, you can celebrate at home. You can also throw the party at a public park, assuming there aren't any regulations against it.

Guest List

The number of guests you invite will depend on how much space you have. Ideally, you'll have a couple of different areas, so that dogs who are getting too rambunctious can either be separated from one another or allowed to play where they won't cause a ruckus. Make sure that your guest list includes dogs that get along well. If, like in most parties, some of the guests will be meeting for the first time, try to leave out fearful dogs whose reaction to meeting a new dog is to bark and carry on. (Those dogs do better at very small

gatherings where they won't be too overwhelmed.)

Introductions

If the canine party guests can be off leash, tensions will be dramatically reduced. Leashes don't allow dogs to go through normal greeting rituals. If the human at the other end of the leash is nervous, it goes right down the leash to the dog.

If at all possible, introduce the dogs off leash (in a safe area, of course). Keep introductions upbeat. Assume all will go well and it probably will, particularly if you've been careful in formulating your guest list. If any particular dogs look tense around one another, separate them, using a happy tone of voice. Remember, everyone is there to have fun!

Menu

Any treat in this book is certainly appropriate for a dog party. The mini-cupcakes and muffins found in this chapter make tasty, easy-to-eat (and serve) party fare. The frozen treats found in Chapter 5 are perfect accompaniments to the cakes. If you'd prefer to make a whole cake, rather than cupcakes, try the liver torte or use the cupcake recipes and just bake them longer.

My friend Gina Barnett made a graduation cake for the puppy class with which she was assisting. She topped it with raw chicken feet sticking out like candles, which certainly caught the attention of the human attendees. Any revulsion they might have felt was replaced by delight as they saw their young dogs chowing down on the feet! Use your imagination in decorating the party food. Remember, though, that decorations are for the humans; the dogs really don't care what the food looks like.

Activities

What would a birthday party be without games? Just use your imagination and you can come up with some great games for all willing participants. Here are some ideas:

· **A tail-wagging contest.** The human gets the dog to wag his or her tail using just tone of voice. The dog with the most wags per minute wins.

· **Bobbing for treats (or toys).** Fill a bucket or a child's wading pool with water. Scatter some treats or toys in the water and let each dog bob for the desired object. If you want to make it a contest, time how long it takes each dog to snag the treat or toy.

· **The shell game.** Bring out three plastic drinking cups and line them up in a row, upside down. Make a big deal of placing a treat under one of the cups. Move the three cups around, changing their positions in the line, while the dog watches. See how long it takes the dog to knock over the cup that's covering the treat.

· **A talent show.** Ask each human party guest to select one trick his or her dog performs well. Sit in a circle and, one at a time, each dog can show off his trick. No need to make this a competition—it can turn into a fun learning experience instead, with each human explaining how the trick was taught.

· **Lessons from a trainer.** If you have a fun, positive-reinforcement-based trainer in town, see about hiring him or her to come to your party for an hour and teach the dogs how to do tricks.

· **"My Dog Can Do That!"** This fun board game has cards with behaviors on it (of varying degrees of difficulty) for the dogs to perform. You make your way around the board, progressing more quickly if your dog is able to do the trick on the card. It comes in a standard-sized board game, which would be a fun party game for a small, indoor party. There's also a trainers' version that has a four-foot-wide floor-mat game board that is fun for outdoor play. It's available from, among other places, www.doglogic.com.

You can find great descriptions of party (and other) games in *Beyond Fetch: Fun Interactive Activities for You and Your Dog*, by D. Caroline Coile, Ph.D.

Party Favors

To make this feel like a real birthday party, it can be fun to send each of your party guests home with party favors. You can bake up a variety of treats from this book and pre-package them to be sent home with your guests, or you can just package up any leftovers on the spot.

It's easy to find inexpensive toys that can make a nice souvenir. A catalog called PetEdge (www.petedge.com) has weekly specials with plush toys selling at remarkably low prices (sometimes under a dollar). You can also buy inexpensive tennis balls for your guests' fetching pleasure.

If you're a crafty type, make bandanas that the guests can wear at the party and take home with them. That will add a festive air to the occasion.

A Party Precaution

Make sure that each of your canine guests has a human escort who stays for the party. Everyone should watch for signs of stress in his or her dog (ears back, quick panting, a general look of unease). When necessary, a stressed dog should be taken away from the group for a little time out. Designating a quiet room where dogs can go to get away from it all (one at a time) might help keep any dog from becoming overwhelmed.

Valentine Heart Sandwiches

These sweet little sandwiches are a great way to tell your dog, "I love you." The strawberry in the cream cheese is just for color (though dogs seem to think it's tasty). You can reverse the colors by putting some raspberries in the cookie batter (or a drop or two of red food coloring) and using plain cream cheese in the middle. Of course, any shape cookie will work, but the heart shape makes a fun Valentine's Day treat.

3 cups all-purpose flour

$1/2$ cup white cornmeal or oat bran

$1/2$ cup grated Parmesan cheese

1 egg, beaten

1 cup of milk

Soft strawberry cream cheese

- Preheat the oven to 350° F.
- Combine the flour, cornmeal or oat bran, and Parmesan cheese in a large bowl. Add the egg and milk. Stir into a soft dough, using your hands to incorporate all the flour. Roll to 1/8-inch thickness. Using a heart-shaped cookie cutter, cut out cookies and place on a baking sheet covered with greased or non-stick foil.
- *Optional:* To ensure that the sandwich cookies don't puff up too much (and thus make the sandwiches too thick), cover them with foil and place another (empty) baking sheet on top of them before putting in oven.
- Bake for 20 minutes or until the tops are brown. Cool on wire rack. Once the cookies are cool, place a small amount of strawberry cream cheese between two cookies to form a sandwich.

Pumpkin Pie Biscuits

These biscuits make your house smell like Thanksgiving! Pumpkin is a great source of fiber. You can add any leftover pumpkin to your dog's food, if you'd like. It makes a great, low-calorie filler. The added spices and syrup make these treats sweet and aromatic.

1$\frac{1}{2}$ cups whole wheat flour

2 cups all-purpose flour, plus extra for rolling

$\frac{1}{2}$ cup rolled oats

1 teaspoon cinnamon

$\frac{1}{2}$ teaspoon nutmeg

$\frac{1}{2}$ cup chicken broth

$\frac{3}{4}$ cup canned pumpkin (not pumpkin pie mix)

1 tablespoon oil

1 tablespoon maple syrup

1 egg

- Preheat the oven to 350° F.

- In a large bowl, combine the dry ingredients. Blend together the broth, pumpkin, oil, syrup, and egg in a blender or food processor. Add the wet ingredients to the dry ingredients and mix together with a spoon. Using your hands, incorporate all the flour into the dough. Roll out onto a floured surface. Lightly sprinkle flour on top of the dough, keeping it floured so it won't stick to the rolling pin. Roll to $\frac{1}{2}$-inch thickness. Cut out the biscuits with cookie cutters and place on a baking sheet covered with greased or non-stick foil. Bake for 30 to 40 minutes or until brown. Store in an airtight container in the refrigerator.

Red and Green Christmas Cookies

These biscuits are slightly more complicated to make than most other recipes in this book, but they're very pretty and make a great gift at holiday time! Hint: To save time, buy pre-washed spinach.

$3^1/4$ **cups all-purpose flour**

1 cup grated Parmesan cheese

$^1/2$ **cup tomato juice**

2 tablespoons safflower oil

$1^1/2$ **cup loosely packed spinach leaves**

$^1/4$ **cup water**

- Preheat the oven to 325° F.

- Blend the flour and cheese in a large bowl. Put $2^1/4$ cups of the flour-cheese mixture into the food processor. Add tomato juice and 1 tablespoon of the oil. Mix together until a ball of red dough forms. Remove the dough from the food processor and set aside.

- Rinse out the food processor bowl. Return it to the base and add spinach. Process to chop the spinach. Add water while the blade is going and continue to process until the spinach is finely chopped. Add the remaining 1 tablespoon of oil and remaining 2 cups of the flour mixture. Process to form green dough.

- On a lightly floured surface, roll red and green dough out, separately, into $^1/4$- inch-thick ovals. Try to make the ovals the same size and shape. Stack the green oval atop the red oval and roll again. Use cookie cutters to cut into Christmas shapes. Place on a baking sheet covered with greased or non-stick foil. Bake 25 to 30 minutes or until just starting to brown on top. Store in an airtight container in the refrigerator.

Liver Birthday Torte

This tasty cake will make a birthday very special! The torte is somewhat flat. If you want a thicker layer cake, double the recipe and pour the batter into two pans. Use the frosting between the layers and on the top. Be sure not to frost until you're ready to serve. Otherwise, the frosting will become blotchy. A little goes a long way with this cake. You might find it easier to cut into small pieces if you bake it in a square pan.

$^1\!/_2$ **cup whole wheat flour**

$^1\!/_2$ **cup rye flour**

$^1\!/_2$ **cup wheat or oat bran**

1 recipe Simple Liver Puree (see page 112)

2 medium carrots or 10 baby carrots

$^1\!/_2$ **cup applesauce**

$^1\!/_4$ **cup olive oil**

1 egg

2 cloves garlic (or 1 teaspoon pre-chopped garlic)

For frosting:

$^1\!/_2$ **cup soft cream cheese**

$1^1\!/_2$ **tablespoons olive or safflower oil**

- Preheat the oven to 350° F. Grease 9-inch round cake pan.

- In a large bowl, combine the flours and bran. Make the Simple Liver Puree. Reserve $^1\!/_4$ cup of the puree. Empty the rest into the bowl with the dry ingredients. Add the carrots to the food processor (don't bother to wash the processor if you've just used it for the puree). Process until finely chopped. Add the applesauce, olive oil, egg, and garlic. Mix together thoroughly. Add this liquid mixture to the flours and liver in the bowl. Mix thoroughly with a spoon. Spoon into the cake pan. Bake for 25 to 30 minutes. Cool on a wire rack. Frost right before serving.

• *For frosting:* Combine the $1/2$ cup soft cream cheese with the $1/4$ cup reserved liver puree. Add the $1^1/2$ tablespoons of olive or safflower oil and mix until smooth. Frost the top of the layer only. Decorate with candles, dog treats, or whatever strikes your fancy. Cut into slices and serve. Store leftovers in the refrigerator in an airtight container.

Carob Cupcakes

Mini muffins tend to be easier to feed to a dog than full-size muffins. If you hand your dog a big muffin, he'll probably make a mess eating it. To make this treat extra delicious, frost with a mixture of cream cheese and liver puree, with a little oil thrown in for spreadability (see Liver Birthday Torte recipe, page 56).

2 cups whole wheat flour

3 tablespoons carob powder

2 teaspoons baking soda

1 egg

$^1/_4$ cup honey

$^3/_4$ cup vanilla (or plain) yogurt

$^1/_2$ cup milk

$^1/_4$ cup safflower oil

- Preheat the oven to 350° F. Line the cups of a muffin tin with paper cups or spray them with oil.
- Mix together dry ingredients in a large bowl. In a smaller bowl, beat the egg and add the honey, yogurt, milk, and safflower oil. Stir together. Add the liquid mixture to the dry ingredients and mix thoroughly to create a thick batter. Spoon into muffin pan, filling each cup three-quarters full.
- Bake regular-sized muffins for 20 to 25 minutes (mini muffins for 10 to 15 minutes) or until a toothpick inserted in the center comes out clean. Store at room temperature in an airtight container for up to three days.

Mini Carrot Cupcakes

Mini-muffins make great bite-sized treats. These dense little cupcakes are fun and easy to serve at a party. Frosting them with cream cheese makes them more festive, but might also make them messier to eat. Be forewarned!

$^3/_4$ **cup whole wheat flour**

$^1/_4$ **cup soy flour**

1 teaspoon baking soda

1 cup ground carrots (18 to 20 baby carrots)

1 egg

$^1/_4$ **cup cottage cheese**

$^1/_4$ **cup safflower oil**

$^1/_3$ **cup honey**

1 teaspoon vanilla

- Preheat the oven to 325° F. Line the cups of a mini-muffin tin with paper cups or spray them with oil.

- Combine the dry ingredients in a large bowl. In a food processor, grind the carrots. Add the egg, cottage cheese, oil, honey, and vanilla and blend together in the food processor. Add the wet mixture to the dry ingredients and stir. Spoon the batter into the muffin cups, filling them about $^3/_4$ full. Bake for 15 minutes, or until a toothpick inserted in the center comes out clean.

- If desired, frost with cream cheese right before serving. Store in the refrigerator in an air-tight container.

Peanut Butter Banana Muffins

You might like to try these muffins yourself. If they appeal to you, try adding a $^1/_2$ teaspoon of salt, which will make them a little more appealing to the human palate.

1 cup all-purpose flour

1 cup whole wheat flour

1 tablespoon baking powder

$^1/_4$ teaspoon salt

$^1/_2$ cup natural peanut butter

1 egg

$^3/_4$ cup milk

1 banana

3 tablespoons oil

$^1/_4$ cup honey or molasses

- Preheat the oven to 400° F. Line the cups of a mini-muffin tin with paper cups or spray them with oil.
- In a large bowl, mix together the dry ingredients and set aside. Blend the peanut butter, egg, and milk together in a food processor. Add the banana and the oil and honey or molasses. Mix until well blended. Fold the wet ingredients into the dry ingredients using a spoon or spatula. Mix just until the dry ingredients are incorporated. Spoon the mixture into the muffin pan, filling each cup about $^3/_4$ full. Bake for 15 minutes or until the tops are brown and a toothpick inserted into center comes out clean. (Regular-sized muffins will need to bake for 25 minutes.) Store at room temperature in an airtight container for up to three days.

Bacon Cheese Muffins

The bacon and cheese in these mini-muffins will make your dog jump for joy. Feel free to use regular muffin tins if you don't have a mini-muffin tin. Regular muffins will be messier, so consider feeding them to your dog outside.

1 cup all-purpose flour

1 cup whole wheat flour

1 tablespoon baking powder

$^1/_4$ teaspoon salt

1 egg

1 cup milk

$^1/_4$ cup honey or molasses

3 tablespoons oil

$^3/_4$ cup cheddar cheese, shredded

$^1/_4$ cup cooked bacon (six slices), drained and crumbled

- Preheat the oven to 400° F. Line the cups of a mini-muffin tin with paper cups or spray them with oil.
- In a large bowl, mix together flours, baking powder, and salt. Make a well in the middle of this dry mixture. In a small bowl, beat the egg with a fork. Add milk, honey or molasses, and oil and stir together. Pour the wet ingredients into the well in the dry ingredients and fold in, stirring until just combined. Gently stir in cheese and bacon. Spoon the mixture into the mini-muffin pan, filling each cup about $^3/_4$ full. Bake for 15 minutes (25 minutes for regular-sized muffins) or until the tops are brown and toothpick inserted into center comes out clean. Store in the refrigerator in an airtight container.

CHAPTER FIVE

Kids and Dogs:
Keeping them Happy and Safe

Those of us who were lucky enough to have grown up with dogs know how important they can be to children. They can become kids' confidants, companions, protectors, and true friends.

When you're preparing treats for your canine family members, it only makes sense to get your kids involved. The no-bake recipes in this chapter are easy and safe for your children to make, under your supervision, of course.

Remember, your kids can help with other recipes in this book, as well. They can be a great help cutting biscuits with cookie cutters, for example. Chapter Two is full of treats that your children can help you with! They might also especially enjoy helping with the holiday treats in Chapter Four.

When your child gives your dog treats, it helps build their bond. Teach your child to offer small treats on the palm of his or her hand, to keep the dog from inadvertently nipping at your child's fingers. The dog-child relationship is about more than treats, of course. It's also about safety and trust.

Safety Through Training

Almost half of the nearly 800,000 people seen by doctors every year for dog bites are children under the age of 13, according to the Centers for Disease Control. Children five to nine years old are the most likely victims.

If you live with both children and dogs, it is your duty to keep your kids safe from any kind of dog-related injury. One way to do this is to train your children to treat your dog (and all dogs) with respect. Your kids should be instructed to never:

• approach a strange dog

• run away from a dog they're afraid of

• hit, kick, or poke a dog

• tease a dog by withholding food

• chase a dog

• pull a dog's tail or ears

• reach through a fence to pet a dog

• try to help an injured dog (get an adult instead)

• take a toy, food, or treat away from a dog

• wake up a sleeping dog

• tease a crated dog

In addition to teaching your kids these important rules, you should take your dog to training classes to teach him or her self-control. A well-trained, well-socialized dog is less likely to bite (though any dog might bite when threatened or in pain).

Socializing Your Dog

If you adopt a puppy, be sure and socialize him or her while young (under four months old). The more things your puppy is exposed to, the fewer things he or she will find frightening as an adult. A confident dog is less likely to bite than a fear-ful one. If you adopt an adult dog and don't know his or her history with children, socialize your new dog just like you would a puppy.

Even if you don't have children of your own, expose your dog to well-behaved children. From a dog's perspective, children are completely different from adults. What's more, a child's face is much closer to a dog's, making a serious bite even easier. Ask well-behaved children to give your dog a treat from their flat palm. Try to do it every time your dog encounters kids. Do it enough and your dog will associate kids with only good things.

Pupsicles

These are an all-natural alternative to the frozen confection made for dogs available in the grocer's freezer aisle. A single look at that product's ingredients list will make you appreciate the short, pronounceable list of ingredients here!

32 ounces low-fat or non-fat yogurt

2 mashed bananas

$^1/_2$ cup natural peanut butter

2 tablespoons honey

- Combine all the ingredients in a bowl. Blend well. Fill small paper cups (like three-ounce bathroom-size paper cups) with mixture. Freeze at least two hours or until solid. To serve, let thaw slightly and pop a Pupsicle out of the cup into a bowl by pressing on the bottom of the cup.

Frozen Chicken Pops

This treat couldn't be easier to make. When your dog is hot, a frozen pop is a real pleasure. Since the treat might melt faster than your dog can eat it, serve it in a bowl (or give it to him outside).

1 cup plain low-fat yogurt

$^1/_2$ cup chicken broth

- Whisk the yogurt and broth together until smooth. Spoon into an ice cube tray. Freeze for at least four hours or until frozen solid. Pop out one cube at a time and serve to your dog on a hot day.

Tuna Frosties

Here's another easy-to-make and tasty summertime treat. For bigger pops, freeze in bathroom-sized paper cups.

1 cup non-fat yogurt

1 (7-ounce) can of tuna packed in water, not drained

- Blend the ingredients together, using a whisk, blender, or immersion blender. Pour into ice cube trays and freeze for at least four hours or until solid. Feed to your dog one cube at a time.

Liver Pupsicles

This treat was created by ace recipe tester and treat maker Amy Heggie. Besides freezing this mixture in cups, you can also stuff it into a Kong® with some training treats, freeze the Kong, and then give it to your dog. This should keep him or her busy licking it out. An adult should do the preparation of the liver puree, which involves boiling and pureeing liver. The kids can get involved after that.

1¼ cups (1 pound), Simple Liver Puree (see page 112)
½ cup low-fat plain yogurt
½ cup canned pumpkin
1 tablespoon minced garlic
Bone-shaped biscuits (of any type)

• An adult should make the Simple Liver Puree. After it's finished, add the yogurt, pumpkin, and garlic to the liver puree and stir until smooth. Pour this mixture into small paper cups (like three-ounce bathroom-size paper cups). Stick a bone-shaped treat into each cup to serve as a handle. Freeze until solid. Push the bottom of the cup to pop out the Pupsicle and serve as a fun treat on a hot day.

Poodle Jellies

Your dog might wonder how to eat this treat at first—it's roughly the same consistency as the gelatin you ate as a kid. However, in short time, he or she will be gobbling it up. If you'd like, you can pour the warm gelatin mixture into ice cube trays and freeze for later use. You can also add goodies to the mix—pieces of cooked chicken or even small cubes of cheese make a great addition.

3 envelopes unflavored gelatin

1 can (14 ounce) chicken broth

- Put one cup of the chicken broth into a saucepan and heat to a boil. Pour the rest of the broth into a bowl and add the gelatin. Do not mix. When the contents of the saucepan have boiled, add hot broth to the bowl and stir until the gelatin is completely dissolved. Pour into an 8 x 8-inch pan and chill in refrigerator until firm.
- When ready to serve, cut the gelatin into squares (or use cookie cutters to cut into fun shapes). If necessary, dip the bottom of the pan into warm water to loosen. Remove the squares/shapes and serve to your surprised dog. Store in the refrigerator in an airtight container.

Peanut Butter Crunch Balls

These treats are easy (and fun) for kids to make. They look so yummy your kids might want to join your dog in enjoying these healthy treats!

1 cup Grape-Nuts® cereal

$^1/_2$ cup wheat bran

$^3/_4$ cup natural peanut butter

$^1/_2$ cup honey

Chopped peanuts (optional)

• Mix the Grape-Nuts and wheat bran together in a large bowl. Add peanut butter and honey and mix well, using your hands to blend the somewhat sticky concoction together. Roll into balls the appropriate size for your dog. You can roll each ball in chopped peanuts for extra crunch, if desired. Chill and serve. Store in the refrigerator in an airtight container.

CHAPTER SIX

For Pudgy Pooches

Let's face it. America is not a country of skinny people. Nor is it populated with skinny dogs. In fact, 25 percent of dogs (and cats) in the western world are obese, according to a 2003 report from the National Research Council.

Being overweight is not healthy for dogs or for humans. It can lead to diabetes, heart problems, even cancer. If you love your dog, make sure you avoid overfeeding him or her.

Is Your Dog Fat?

Sometimes it's hard to tell that your dog is getting fat—these things tend to sneak up on us. One way to determine if your dog is overweight is the rib test. Feel your dog's sides. You should be able to feel ribs without pushing hard. If you have to dig around with your fingers to feel any ribs, it's time to start thinking about putting your dog on a diet. Another way to tell if your dog is fat is to look at his or her waistline and "abdominal tuck." The abdomens of most healthy dogs tuck up behind the rib cage. If your dog has a saggy belly, it's time to think about cutting back on those treats. (If your dog's belly is distended or drum-like, see your veterinarian, as this can be a sign of serious illness.)

Weight-Loss Tips

It can be just as hard to help your dog lose weight as it is to lose weight yourself. Dogs love to eat. We love to feed them. You wouldn't be reading this book if you didn't enjoy giving your dog treats, and there's nothing wrong with that.

The key—as in most things—is moderation. You can feed your dog lower-calorie treats, like those found in this chapter. You can also feed him or her smaller treats. Break a biscuit into four pieces and give your dog one piece at a time throughout the day, rather than four biscuits a day. If your dog is small, cut those training treats into pieces the size of an infant's pinkie fingernail. The act of giving (and receiving) is an important part of giving your dog a treat. The size of the treat is incidental.

Reducing the amount of treats you give your dog probably won't be enough for any major weight loss, however. You have to cut back on your dog's food. (If your dog is grossly overweight, talk with your veterinarian before starting a weight-loss program.) Naturally, when you cut back on your dog's food, he or she might still feel hungry. Your once well-behaved pooch might become a counter surfer or garbage raider. One way to get around this is to add some low-calorie bulk to the reduced ration of food. Adding canned pumpkin (not pumpkin pie mix) and vegetables (if your dog will eat them) to your dog's food are good ways to help your dog feel full. If you're feeding a home-prepared diet, try increasing the proportion of vegetables in the food.

Low-cal treats will also help stave off hunger. Feeling hungry all the time is no fun for dog or human. Just be judicious about the quantity of food you feed at meals and cut back on between-meal snacks. Make sure the snacks you do feed are low in fat (and therefore in calories) like the ones in this chapter. High fiber snacks (like those found in Chapter Eight) can also help your dog feel full.

You don't have to limit yourself to the treats

in this chapter. One way to cut down on calories in a treat recipe is to cut back on the fat content. It's easy to modify recipes to lower the fat in them. Some possibilities include substituting applesauce for oil, or using non-fat milk in place of whole or low-fat milk. You can also use non-fat broths and cheese when a recipe calls for one of those ingredients. Substitute two egg whites for one whole egg.

Remember that fat in and of itself isn't a bad thing. Dogs (and humans) need a certain amount of fat in their diets. With treats, which are admittedly extras, cutting back on fat is a good idea.

If you're reducing your dog's treat intake, make sure you enlist the help of the whole family. It won't do your dog any good if your kids or spouse are giving him or her food on the sly!

Exercise Is Important, Too

Of course, the other side of the weight-loss coin is exercise. Many pudgy pooches simply don't get enough. If yours is one of them, check with your vet first, then put your dog on an exercise regimen. Simply lengthening the walks you take your dog on will help both of you become more physically fit. Don't discount the importance of playing together. It burns calories while building the bond between the two of you and it's fun!

If your dog has achy joints, exercise might be painful. Being overweight makes joint pain even worse. Swimming might help provide non-weight-bearing exercise until the pounds start to drop off and your dog's joints become less painful. Again, check with your vet first before starting a vigorous exercise program, particularly if your dog has a lot of weight to lose or is stiff and sore. Your vet might be able to offer some safe, natural relief for those painful joints with glucosamine/chondroitin compounds or other joint supplements.

The Thyroid Connection

If your dog isn't losing weight even after you've cut down on the amount you're feeding, a vet check is definitely in order. Dogs who eat little but stay fat might have a poorly functioning thyroid gland. This is known as hypothyroidism, which is common among dogs. In fact, it's the most common canine endocrine disorder.

When you ask your veterinarian to check your dog's thyroid levels, be sure to ask for a complete thyroid profile. Veterinarian and researcher Jean Dodds, DVM, who is an expert in thyroid problems, suggests this include the following tests: total T4, total T3, free T4, free T3, TSH, and circulating T4 and T3 autoantibodies. According to Dr. Dodds, a simple T4 measurement (a common thyroid test) is not sufficient for diagnosis of hypothyroidism.

If your dog is diagnosed with hypothyroidism, your veterinarian will doubtless prescribe a synthetic (and inexpensive) thyroid hormone, which should help him or her lose excess weight—and feel peppier.

Low-Fat Cream Cheese Biscuits

These treats are low in fat, but still tasty! If you prefer, you can crush fresh garlic cloves and sprinkle them on top of the batter, rather than using garlic powder. Two or three cloves will be sufficient.

$1^1/_2$ cups whole wheat flour, plus extra for rolling

$^1/_3$ cup oatmeal

3 ounces non-fat cream cheese

$^1/_3$ cup applesauce

$^1/_3$ cup water

Garlic powder for sprinkling

• Preheat the oven to 375° F.

• Combine the flour and oatmeal in a large bowl. Place the cream cheese, applesauce, and water in a food processor and mix until the cream cheese is liquefied. Pour the cheese/applesauce mixture into the dry ingredients and mix. Knead into a dough, adding extra flour, if necessary, to ensure that the dough isn't too sticky to roll out. Turn the dough out onto a lightly floured surface. Roll dough to about $^1/_4$-inch thickness and sprinkle with garlic powder (or fresh garlic), if desired. Cut into shapes with cookie cutters. Place cookies on a baking sheet covered with greased or non-stick foil. Bake for 20 minutes. Store in the refrigerator in an airtight container.

Herbalicious Biscuits

The herbs in this low-fat and high-fiber biscuit make it more flavorful, but if it's not zippy enough for your dog, sprinkle some non-fat cheese on top of the cookies before baking and forego the glaze. You needn't limit yourself to the herbs mentioned—feel free to use any culinary herbs you think your dog will like (or that you have in your pantry).

$2^1/2$ cups whole wheat flour, plus extra for rolling

$1^1/4$ cups cornmeal

2 teaspoons garlic powder

1 teaspoon dried dill

1 teaspoon dried rosemary

1 teaspoon dried parsley

1 teaspoon dried mint

1 teaspoon dried oregano

$1^1/4$ cup water

1 egg white for glazing

- Preheat the oven to 375° F.
- In a large bowl, blend all dry ingredients. Add water and knead into dough. Turn dough out onto a lightly floured surface. Roll to 1/4-inch thickness and cut with cookie cutters. Place cookies on a baking sheet covered with greased or non-stick foil. For glaze, brush the beaten egg white on top of each cookie. Bake for 25 to 35 minutes or until the tops are browned. For crispier biscuits, turn the oven down to 200° F and bake for another hour. Store at room temperature in a loosely covered container.

Pumpkin Drop Cookies

Pumpkin is low in calories and high in fiber—and it tastes good, making it great for pudgy pooches. This treat is low in fat and tasty enough to make your dog ask for more. Hint: Use small cookie cutters for small treats that will satisfy your dog's taste buds without overdoing the calories.

$1^1/2$ **cups whole wheat flour**

$^1/2$ **teaspoon ground cinnamon**

$^1/2$ **teaspoon ground nutmeg**

3 tablespoons applesauce

2 egg whites

$^1/2$ **cup solid-pack pumpkin**

1 tablespoon molasses

$^1/2$ **cup water**

- Preheat the oven to 400° F.
- Combine all ingredients in a large bowl and mix together to a cookie-dough-like consistency. Drop by the teaspoonful, 1 inch apart, onto a greased baking sheet. Bake for 12 to 15 minutes or until cookies are firm. For harder cookies, turn off the oven and let cookies cool in the oven, 1 to 2 hours or overnight. Store in the refrigerator in an airtight container.

Low-Fat Carrot Biscuits

The carrots in these cookies pack a wallop in terms of flavor, without packing in the calories. This treat is very moist thanks to the high moisture content of the carrots.

4 cups whole wheat flour, plus more as needed

$1/2$ cup oat or wheat bran

$1/4$ cup non-fat dry milk

$1/2$ cup ground carrots (9 to 10 baby carrots)

1 cup non-fat chicken broth

$1/2$ cup unsweetened applesauce

2 egg whites

- Preheat the oven to 375° F.
- Combine flour, oat bran, and dry milk in a large bowl. In a food processor, grind the carrots. Add the chicken broth, applesauce, and egg whites to the food processor and mix. Add the liquid mixture to the dry mixture and stir into a soft dough. Knead it in the bowl, adding up to a half cup more flour, as needed, to make the dough less sticky. Turn out onto a floured surface and sprinkle the dough with flour. Roll to $1/4$- to $1/2$-inch thickness and cut into shapes with cookie cutters. Prick each treat with a fork, to prevent it from puffing up too much. Place the treats on a baking sheet covered with greased or non-stick foil and bake for 15 to 20 minutes, or until the tops brown. Store in the refrigerator in an airtight container.

Oatmeal Garlic Cookies

Small is good when it comes to drop cookies. Make the cookies smaller than you think you need to so that your dog can eat one in a single bite. Otherwise, you'll be vacuuming up crumbs!

$2^{1}/_{4}$ **cups whole wheat flour**

1 cup uncooked oatmeal

$^{1}/_{2}$ **cup oat bran**

$^{1}/_{2}$ **cup non-fat dry milk**

4 cloves garlic, minced (or 1 tablespoon of pre-minced garlic)

2 eggs, beaten

$^{1}/_{3}$ **cup applesauce**

1 cup non-fat chicken broth

- Preheat the oven to 325° F.
- Mix together the dry ingredients in a large bowl. Add the garlic, eggs, applesauce, and chicken broth and stir well. Drop in small rounded teaspoonfuls onto a baking sheet covered with greased or non-stick foil. Bake for 25 to 30 minutes, until the tops are brown. Store in the refrigerator in an airtight container.

CHAPTER SEVEN

Grain-Free Treats

Chances are, your dog eats a lot of grains. If you're feeding kibble, it's a given. Dry dog food is made primarily from grains, after all. So are most dog biscuits. Nowadays, a growing number of people are avoiding feeding grains to their dogs. These include people with itchy dogs, dogs with cancer, or raw feeders who feel that grains are an unnatural part of a dog's diet.

If you fall into one of these categories, you don't have to avoid treats in order to avoid grains. The recipes in this chapter either avoid flour altogether or call for flours that aren't derived from grains, like soy flour, garbanzo bean flour, and tapioca flour. Other non-grain flours include potato flour, arrowroot flour, almond flour, chestnut flour, and water chestnut flour. In addition, flours made from unusual, ancient grains like amaranth and quinoa can be used sparingly for itchy dogs, who probably haven't been exposed to them before and most likely have not developed a sensitivity to them. These types of flours are available in large supermarkets and health food stores. A popular brand is Bob's Red Mill, which sells its products on its website (www.bobsredmill.com) as well as in stores.

Itchy Dogs

Itchy dogs—the ones who lick their paws a lot and have itchy ears—may be reacting to grains in their diet. Some people find that eliminating grains in their dogs' diets helps make their dogs more comfortable. Often in addition to eliminating grains, they'll add fatty acids or other dietary supplements.

If your dog is itchy, going grain-free is an avenue worth exploring. Unless you're feeding a prescription anti-allergy diet (like Hill's z/d), you'll probably have to switch to a home-prepared diet (or a pre-packaged raw diet) to avoid grains. Don't make such a switch without doing appropriate research, however. Read books, talk with other dog owners experienced in feeding home-prepared diets, and seek the help of your veterinarian (though you may have to consult with a holistic veterinarian) before taking the plunge and starting a home-prepared diet.

See Appendix Three for a list of books regarding raw diets.

If you're already feeding grain-free, the recipes in this chapter can give you some more treat options. You can also adapt any of the other recipes by using grain-free flours. The result might be different, but your dog will probably enjoy it!

Dogs with Cancer

Studies by veterinary researcher Dr. Greg Ogilvie when he was at Colorado State University, indicate that dogs with cancer should avoid simple carbohydrates found in grains. Cancer cells gobble up carbohydrates, so limiting them helps starve cancer. If your dog has been diagnosed with cancer and you're feeding dry dog food (which is grain-based) talk with your veterinarian about a diet change if it hasn't already come up. At least one canned prescription diet, Hill's canine n/d, is formulated for dogs with cancer, based on Dr. Ogilvie's research. You can learn more about Dr. Ogilvie's recommendations through the resources listed in Appendix Three. The grain-free treats in this section will allow you to bake treats for your dog without fear of promoting cancer growth.

Raw-Fed Dogs

A growing number of pet owners are feeding their dogs a raw diet, usually comprised of raw, meaty bones, raw muscle and organ meat, and raw, pulverized vegetables. While there are a variety of opinions on what constitutes the best raw diet, no one diet is perfect for all dogs. Individual dogs have individual dietary needs (and tastes).

Many raw feeders feel that grains are an unnatural component of a dog's diet and do not feed them. Some dogs do especially well without grains. My own dogs (and cat) eat a raw diet; grains are not usually a part of their meals. I do, however, make them grain-based treats, and they also enjoy the grain-free treats from this chapter of the book.

Grain-Free Liver Crunchies

If you want a crunchy treat that you can store on the counter, bake these treats twice, just like biscotti.
For a nice soft training treat, stop after the first baking.

1 pound (2 cups) beef liver

2 eggs

1¹/₂ cups garbanzo bean flour

¹/₂ cup cheddar cheese, shredded

- Preheat the oven to 300° F.
- Puree the liver with the eggs in a food processor. Add this mixture to the flour in a large bowl and stir in the cheese. Mix well and turn out onto a baking sheet covered with greased or non-stick foil. Bake for 25 minutes or until firm on top.
- Remove from the oven and cool. When cool enough to handle, turn the dough over, peel off the foil and cut into training-treat-sized treats. For soft treats, refrigerate the treats or freeze any you won't be using within a week. For crunchy, biscotti-like treats, return the cut treats to the oven and bake at 150° F for three hours or until treats are hard and crunchy. Twice-baked treats can be stored at room temperature in a loosely covered container.

Grain-Free Cheese Biscuits

Garbanzo bean flour is just one of several types of non-grain flours that are readily available in health food stores (and some larger supermarkets). You can substitute others of these flours, keeping an eye on the consistency of the dough. If you're not limiting grains, feel free to use wheat flour in this recipe.

3 cups garbanzo bean flour, plus extra as necessary and for rolling

$1/4$ cup powdered milk

1 cup cheddar cheese

2 tablespoons safflower oil

$3/4$ cup warm water

Grated Parmesan cheese for topping

- Preheat the oven to 375° F.

- Mix the flour, powdered milk, and cheddar cheese together in a bowl. Add oil and water. Stir into a dough. Add some more flour (up to $1/4$ cup) if the dough is too sticky to roll out easily. Turn the dough out onto a lightly floured surface and roll to $1/4$- to $1/2$-inch thickness, putting flour on the rolling pin, if necessary. Sprinkle with Parmesan cheese. Cut into shapes with cookie cutters and place on an ungreased baking sheet. Bake for 10 to 15 minutes or until the tops start to brown. Store in the refrigerator in an airtight container.

Soy Training Dots

These aren't glamorous-looking treats, but they're easy to make and a hit with most dogs.

2 (2.5-ounce) jars of meat baby food

1 egg

$^1/_2$ cup soy flour

$^1/_4$ cup grated Parmesan cheese

• Preheat the oven to 350° F.

• Combine all the ingredients in a bowl and mix with a spoon into a thick batter. Cover a baking sheet with greased or non-stick foil. Spoon the batter into a plastic bag and force the contents into one corner of the bag, twisting the top of the bag to seal. Snip the corner of the plastic bag $^1/_8$-inch tip (or use a pastry bag with a $^1/_4$-inch tip). Squeeze the bag to dispense bite-size dabs of the batter onto the baking sheet. Repeat until all the batter has been dispensed. Bake for 20 minutes or until firm to the touch. Store in the refrigerator in an airtight container.

Salmon Blondies

This fishy, cheesy treat is sure to make your dog's tail wag. It also breaks up very easily, so you could take a few with you on a walk and break off tiny training treats to reward good behavior. If you prefer, you can use a pizza cutter at the outset to cut them into tiny treats.

1 (14.5-ounce) can of salmon, or 2 (7-ounce) cans

$^1/_2$ cup cottage cheese

$1^1/_2$ cups garbanzo bean flour

$^1/_2$ cup shredded cheddar cheese

Grated Parmesan cheese for topping

- Preheat the oven to 350° F.
- Empty can(s) of salmon (liquid, bones, and all) into a food processor. Add cottage cheese and process well, until mixture is a mousse-like consistency. Add flour and cheddar and mix into a sticky, loose dough. Grease the bottom and sides of an 8 x 8- or 12 x 9-inch baking pan. (You'll get thicker blondies with the smaller pan.) Turn dough out into the greased pan and push to the edges of the pan with wet hands or a spatula. Sprinkle with Parmesan cheese. Bake for 35 to 40 minutes or until golden brown. Cool in the pan and then cut into the desired size. Store in the refrigerator in an airtight container.

Ancient Grains Parmesan Twists

These treats aren't technically grain-free. However, chances are good that your dog hasn't been exposed to the grains called for in this recipe and thus hasn't formed an allergy to them. These grains don't smell like wheat flour. Be prepared for an unusual (though not necessarily unpleasant) smell to waft out of your oven!

$1^{1}/_{2}$ **cups amaranth flour, plus extra for rolling**

$1^{1}/_{2}$ **cups quinoa flour**

$^{1}/_{2}$ **teaspoon salt**

$^{1}/_{2}$ **cup grated Parmesan cheese**

2 eggs, beaten

$^{3}/_{4}$ **cup milk**

• Preheat the oven to 325° F.

• In a large bowl, mix together the flours, salt, and $^{1}/_{4}$ cup of the Parmesan cheese. Add the beaten eggs and milk. Mix into a soft dough. If the dough feels sticky, knead some more flour into it, or chill it before working with it. Turn the dough out onto a floured surface. Use your hands or a rolling pin to flatten the dough to $^{1}/_{2}$-inch thickness. Sprinkle with the remaining $^{1}/_{4}$ cup of Parmesan cheese.

• Using a pizza cutter or knife, cut $^{1}/_{2}$-inch-wide strips length-wise. Then make perpendicular cuts, forming strips that are 3 to 4 inches long. Twist each strip several times before placing on a baking sheet covered with greased or non-stick foil. Bake for 25 minutes or until the treats just start to brown. Store in the refrigerator in an airtight container.

CHAPTER EIGHT

Treats for Special-Needs Dogs

Many dogs have or develop special dietary needs, especially as they age. Food sensitivities or chronic illnesses might require that special attention be paid to diet. If you have a special-needs dog, it doesn't mean he or she can't have any treats. You just need to pay close attention to what you dole out. Making your own treats makes that much easier. No longer will you have to scrutinize the ingredients list on commercial treat packages.

The recipes in this chapter address a few of those needs, including high-fiber treats (good for dogs with diabetes and certain gastrointestinal disorders, as well as overweight dogs); low-protein treats (for some dogs with kidney and liver disease); and bland treats (for dogs with a restricted diet due to gastrointestinal problems).

If you have a dog with special dietary needs, you don't have to limit yourself to this chapter of the book. You can adapt the ingredients of other recipes in the book to accommodate your dog's needs. Remember, dogs are highly forgiving, as are the recipes in this book. Since dogs are pretty easy to please flavor-wise, and they don't care about appearance, have fun experimenting with the recipes throughout this book to turn any recipe into one appropriate for your special-needs dog.

High-Fiber Treats

High-fiber treats are filling, so a little goes a long way—which is great for dogs who need to lose some weight. A high-fiber diet is also often recommended for dogs with diabetes and those with intestinal disorders. Fiber helps bulk up the stool, which can be helpful for dogs that have problems with their anal glands. (A firm stool helps dogs express their anal glands without human assistance.) In addition, dogs that have chronic problems with worms can benefit from a high-fiber diet—the bulk can help sweep the worms out. If your vet recommends that you increase the fiber in your dog's diet, these treats can be a tasty part of his diet.

Low-Protein Treats

If your dog has been diagnosed with kidney or liver disease, you may be instructed to feed him a low-protein diet. (Some veterinarians, however, are recommending a diet based on high-quality protein for kidney and liver patients, rather than one low in protein.) Grain-heavy, low-protein treats are easy to make, though the tricky part is making them delicious, since meat and cheese proteins often add flavor to dog treats.

Geriatric dogs often have kidney issues—or at least the potential for them, as their kidneys gradually wear out. Your veterinarian might recommend that you limit your dog's protein intake (even if you're not asked to put your dog on a special low-protein diet). The low-protein recipes in this book allow you to give your dog treats without worrying about increasing his or her protein intake.

Bland Treats

Dogs with temporary diarrhea, or those with chronic intestinal difficulties, are often put on a bland diet. The goal is to not irritate the digestive tract. When your dog has been ill in the past, you may have been asked by your veterinarian to feed him or her boiled hamburger and rice, or chicken and rice. Your dog's gastrointestinal tract doesn't have to work hard to digest this bland food, which helps it recover.

Rather than withholding all treats when your dog is on a bland diet, you can give him or her bland treats (sparingly, just to be careful). The recipes here call for tapioca flour. Tapioca, made from the root of the cassava plant, becomes gelatinous when cooked and is easy to digest. Eggs are also extremely easy for dogs to digest.

If your dog is on a prescription bland diet (like Hill's i/d), examine the label and see if you can formulate a recipe using only ingredients on that list. Using ingredients like rice and meat baby food, it's not hard to do. One way to make treats for dogs on a prescription diet is to use the food itself as an ingredient. If you're feeding a prescription kibble, you can make "flour" out of it by grinding it in a food processor. Mix this "flour" with the other ingredients, like meat baby food in the appropriate flavor, or eggs, to hold it together. Roll it out and cut it with cookie cutters. If you're feeding a canned prescription food, you can make a treat out of it by spooning tiny spots of food onto a foil-covered baking sheet and baking it in a 350° F oven until firm. (You might want to open the windows during baking!)

Just because your dog has special dietary needs doesn't mean he or she has to avoid treats altogether. Still, if your dog is on a strict diet, run the recipe by your veterinarian to be safe.

Apple Bran Muffins

You might want to eat some of these high-fiber muffins yourself! If you have a mini-muffin tin, you'll find the smaller muffins a little easier to feed to your dog.

2 cups whole wheat flour

$1^{1}/_{2}$ cups cornmeal

$^{1}/_{2}$ cup oat or wheat bran

$^{1}/_{2}$ teaspoon baking powder

$^{1}/_{2}$ teaspoon cinnamon

$^{1}/_{2}$ teaspoon nutmeg

1 egg, beaten

$^{2}/_{3}$ cup honey

1 cup applesauce

$1^{1}/_{3}$ cup water

Extra oat bran or rolled oats (optional)

• Preheat the oven to 350° F. Line the cups of a muffin tin with paper cups or spray them with oil.

• In a large bowl, mix the dry ingredients together thoroughly. In a medium bowl, whisk together wet ingredients. Gently fold wet ingredients into dry ingredients until just combined. Spoon batter into cups, filling to $^{2}/_{3}$ full. Sprinkle with oat bran or rolled oats, if desired. Bake for 30 minutes for mini muffins or 40 minutes for regular-sized muffins, or until golden brown. Store at room temperature in an airtight container for up to three days.

High-Fiber Liver Training Treats

This training treat is cakey and very easy to break into little pieces for frequent rewards during a training session. The white bean and rye flours, as well as the flax seed meal, are dense with fiber.

1 pound (2 cups) beef liver

3 eggs

$^1/_2$ cup canned pumpkin

$^1/_2$ cup non-fat ricotta cheese

$^1/_4$ cup olive oil

1 cup whole wheat flour

1 cup rye flour

$^1/_2$ cup white bean flour

$^1/_4$ cup flax seed meal

- Preheat the oven to 400° F.
- Puree the beef liver in the food processor. Add eggs and blend. Add pumpkin, ricotta, and olive oil and blend until thoroughly mixed. In a large bowl, combine flours and flax seed meal. Add the liquid mixture to the dry mixture and stir with a spoon into a sticky dough. Turn out onto a baking sheet covered with grease or non-stick foil. Use a spoon, spatula, or your hands to push the dough to the edges of the baking sheet. Bake for 20 minutes or until the tops are firm and bottoms are browned.
- Allow the treats to cool on the baking sheet. When cool enough to handle, turn the dough over, peel off the foil and cut into small treats. Store in the refrigerator in an airtight container.

Chicken-Tomato Biscuits

If you don't have any tomato juice on hand, you can run crushed tomatoes through the food processor. A little garlic sprinkled on top of these high-fiber treats, along with the Parmesan cheese, would make them even more flavorful.

1$^1/_4$ cups rye flour, plus extra for rolling

1 cup whole wheat flour

1 cup white bean flour

$^1/_4$ cup flax seed meal

$^1/_2$ cup tomato juice

$^1/_2$ cup chicken broth

1 egg, beaten

$^1/_4$ cup grated Parmesan cheese

• Preheat the oven to 375° F.

• Combine the flours and flax seed meal in a large bowl. Add the juice, broth, and egg. Stir together and knead until dough is formed. If necessary, knead in a little extra flour so that the dough is easy to roll out without sticking. Turn out onto a floured surface and sprinkle flour on top of the dough. Roll to $^1/_2$-inch thickness. Sprinkle with Parmesan cheese. Cut into shapes with cookie cutters and place on an ungreased baking sheet. Bake for 20 minutes or until the tops are brown. Store in the refrigerator in an airtight container.

Multigrain Herb Biscuits

This recipe is not only low in protein it is also low in fat and high in fiber. On top of that, it's flavorful, thanks to the herbs. It's one of the few recipes in this book that uses cornmeal. If your dog has a sensitivity to corn, as many dogs do, just substitute a different flour or use wheat or oat bran.

1 teaspoon (about $^1/_2$ package) dry yeast

$^1/_2$ teaspoon molasses

$^1/_4$ cup warm water

2 cups whole wheat flour, plus extra for rolling

1 cup oat flour

1 cup cornmeal

$^1/_4$ cup wheat germ

2 tablespoons mint flakes

2 tablespoons parsley flakes

$1^1/_4$ cup plus 2 tablespoons water

- Preheat the oven to 350° F.
- Combine yeast, molasses, and warm water and let sit five minutes.
- Blend together flours, cornmeal, wheat germ, mint, and parsley. Add yeast mixture and remaining water. Stir until well combined. Turn the dough out onto a lightly floured surface and knead briefly. Roll to $^1/_4$-inch thickness and cut with cookie cutters. Place biscuits on a baking sheet covered with greased or non-stick foil. Bake for about 30 minutes or until light brown and firm. Store at room temperature in a loosely covered container.

Carob Brownies

While chocolate can be toxic to dogs, carob is safe (and low in protein). Plus, most dogs like the flavor, though perhaps not as much as most people like chocolate! Cleaning up will be even easier if you line the pan with greased or non-stick foil before adding the batter.

$1^1/2$ **cups whole wheat flour**

$^1/2$ **cup tapioca flour**

$^1/4$ **cup carob powder**

2 tablespoons applesauce

1 tablespoon brown rice syrup or molasses

1 cup water

- Preheat the oven to 350° F.
- Mix the dry ingredients together in a large bowl. Add applesauce, brown rice syrup or molasses, and water. Use a spoon to mix into a batter. Pour the batter into a greased 8 x 8-inch square baking pan. Use the back of a wet spoon to spread evenly to the edges. Bake for 20 minutes or until the top is firm. Store in the refrigerator in an airtight container.

Low-Protein Garlic Biscuits

Most dogs tend to love protein (especially protein derived from meat). Even so, our canine taste testers really enjoyed this low-protein biscuit!

2 cups barley flour, plus extra for rolling

2 cloves (1 teaspoon pre-chopped) minced or crushed garlic

$1/4$ cup safflower oil

1 teaspoon molasses

$1/3$ cup water

Garlic powder

- Preheat the oven to 350° F.
- Mix the flour and garlic in a large bowl. Add the oil, molasses, and water. Stir together, then knead into a dough. Turn out onto a lightly floured surface. Roll out to $1/4$-inch thickness and sprinkle the dough with garlic powder. Use cookie cutters to cut into shapes, and place on an ungreased baking sheet. Bake for 15 to 20 minutes or until the tops and bottoms start to brown. For crispier treats, turn the oven down to 200° F and bake the biscuits for another hour. Store at room temperature in a loosely covered container.

Chicken Gummy Squares

These bland treats are odd—there's no way around it. They're dense and gummy and dogs think they're delicious. If your dog is on a bland diet, these digestible treats shouldn't upset his or her stomach. They make great snacks or training treats.

1 cup white rice flour

$1/2$ cup tapioca flour

3 (2.5-ounce) jars chicken baby food

$1/4$ cup low-fat yogurt

1 egg

- Preheat the oven to 400° F.
- In a large bowl, mix all ingredients together into a batter. Spoon the batter into a greased 8 x 8-inch pan. Bake for 25 minutes or until the top is brown. Cool thoroughly before cutting into brownie-sized squares or tiny training treats. Store in the refrigerator in an airtight container.

Sensitive Tummy Treats

If your dog is on a bland diet for stomach upset, the gentle ingredients in this treat shouldn't cause any digestive difficulties. These treats are so easy to make, your kids can probably do it without your assistance.

1 (2.5-ounce) jar of chicken or turkey baby food

¹/₂ cup puffed rice (from the breakfast cereal aisle)

• In a medium bowl, mix together the two ingredients. Make small balls by taking a pinch of the mixture and rolling it on your palm. Place on waxed paper or non-stick foil. Chill in the refrigerator for at least two hours. Store in an airtight container in the refrigerator or freeze and serve thawed or frozen.

CHAPTER NINE

Miscellaneous Treats (with a Purpose)

The hodgepodge of treats in this chapter all have one thing in common: each has a function. There are biscuits whose ingredients help ward off fleas, freshen canine breath, give your dog an energy boost, or even help with carsickness. In addition, this chapter includes three treats that, in conjunction with a hollow Kong® toy, will help keep your dog occupied. Finally, there's a simple recipe for a liver puree with a multitude of uses.

Herbs in Treats

Dried and fresh herbs have a variety of medicinal functions. If you're interested in learning more about using herbs for your pet, invest in the beautiful and information-rich coffee-table book, *All You Ever Wanted to Know About Herbs for Pets*, by Mary L. Wulff-Tilford and Gregory L. Tilford.

An easy way to get dogs to eat herbs is to bake them in treats. This chapter has four herb-related treats: two can help freshen breath with herbs like mint, parsley, and dill; one uses dried ginger to ward off nausea in the car; another utilizes celery seed and dried dill, along with garlic and brewer's yeast, to repel fleas.

Treats as Pacifiers

If you share your home with a young dog or an especially active adult dog, you know how important exercise is. Active dogs who are left alone all day—even if they're well exercised—should be left with things to occupy them. This can prevent a lot of damage to household belongings.

One way you can provide this sort of "environmental enrichment" is to leave toys stuffed with food. One favorite such toy is called a Kong. It's a hollow rubber toy shaped like the top of a soft-serve ice cream cone. It has a big hole in the bottom and a small air hole at the top. If you fill an appropriate-sized

Kong with treats and seal up the bottom hole with something sticky like cream cheese or peanut butter, your dog can get worn out trying to get to the treats. Some people even feed their dogs meals this way!

If you want to make it especially challenging for your dog, stuff the Kong, seal it up and freeze it. Your dog will have to work really hard to get the treats out. Any training treat will do the trick. Use your imagination and stuff anything edible inside the Kong—pieces of banana, bits of cheese, even yogurt. Just don't make it too messy! (The Kong company offers Kong-stuffing recipes on its website, www.kongcompany.com.)

In this chapter, you'll find three great recipes for treats that are especially good for stuffing in Kongs. The Meaty Kong Stuffer is a tasty soft treat that you can make whatever size you want (making it easier or harder to remove from the Kong). The Liver Kong bars are dense brownie-like treats you can cut into just the right size to stuff into the Kong. The Liver Kong Filler is a liquid concoction that can ooze between the treats inside your Kong. It makes Kongs especially tough to unstuff when frozen. You can even use all these treats together in one Kong, if you'd like! Of course, any training treat or biscuit can be put inside a Kong.

One company, Pro Active Pet Products, is developing an automatic Kong dispenser that will hold up to five Kongs. Stuff your Kongs in the morning, put them in the machine, and they'll be dispensed at random times throughout the day.

A Treat for the Power Dog

If your dog is active and you're out on the road with him or her, maybe participating in dog sports or just hiking, the chicken performance treats in this chapter can give your dog an energy boost. They're calorie-dense and made with extra fat and protein.

Couldn't Be More Simple—Or More Useful

The final recipe in this chapter is for Simple Liver Puree, which is nothing more than cooked, pureed liver. Your dog probably wouldn't mind being fed an entire bowl of the stuff, but it's really meant to be used in other recipes. You can use it in place of meat baby food in recipes. You can make it ahead of time, freeze it, and use it in recipes that call for pureed liver. You can seal up a Kong with it or coat pills with it to make them easier for your dog to take. Use your imagination and I'm sure you'll find Simple Liver Puree coming in handy all the time.

Fresh and Tasty Herb Biscuits

Unless you have easy access to fresh herbs, you might want to double this recipe to make the most of your herb purchase. Your dog might be a little surprised by the strong aroma and flavor of these treats, but since the herbs have breath-freshening qualities, they can result in sweeter-smelling breath!

2 cups whole-wheat flour, plus extra for rolling

$^1/_2$ cup wheat or oat bran

$^1/_4$ cup grated Parmesan cheese

$^1/_4$ cup fresh parsley

2 tablespoons fresh dill

$^1/_2$ cup chicken broth

2 tablespoons safflower oil

1 egg

- Preheat the oven to 400° F.
- Combine dry ingredients in large bowl. Liquefy the parsley, dill, and chicken broth in a food processor. Add oil and egg to the processor and mix thoroughly. Add liquid mixture to dry ingredients and mix well into a soft dough. Turn out onto a lightly floured surface and roll to $^1/_2$-inch thickness. Use cookie cutters to cut into shapes and place on a baking sheet covered with greased or non-stick foil. Bake for 10 to 15 minutes or until brown. Store in the refrigerator in an airtight container.

Minty Fresh Biscuits

These biscuits can actually help freshen your dog's breath—but don't expect miracles!

1¹/₂ cups all-purpose flour, plus extra for rolling

1 cup whole wheat flour

¹/₂ cup grated Parmesan cheese

3 tablespoons mint flakes

1 egg

³/₄ cup milk

¹/₃ cup olive oil

$$\frac{3 \times 3}{3 \times 4} + \frac{1 \times 4}{3 \times 4} = \frac{9}{12} + \frac{4}{12} = \frac{13}{12} \qquad 1\frac{1}{12}$$

- Preheat the oven to 350° F.

- In a large bowl, mix together the dry ingredients. In a smaller bowl, beat the egg and add milk and oil. Mix together and pour into dry ingredients. Stir together, then knead to incorporate all the flour. Turn out onto a lightly floured surface and roll to ¹/₄- to ¹/₂-inch thickness. Cut into shapes with cookie cutters and place on a baking sheet covered with greased or non-stick foil. Bake for 10 to 15 minutes or until the tops start to brown. If you want crunchier biscuits, turn off the oven and let the biscuits cool 2 or more hours inside the oven or until they're crunchy. Store in the refrigerator in an airtight container. (Hardened biscuits can be stored in a loosely covered container at room temperature.)

Canine Carsickness Cookies

Ginger is a great digestive herb that can help settle the stomach. If your dog tends to get motion sickness in the car, giving him or her one or two of these cookies before a trip can help prevent nausea.

$2^{1}/_{2}$ **cups all-purpose flour**

$^{1}/_{2}$ **cup soy flour**

1 teaspoon baking soda

1 tablespoon powdered ginger

1 egg

$^{1}/_{4}$ **cup honey**

$^{3}/_{4}$ **cup applesauce**

$^{1}/_{4}$ **cup safflower or canola oil**

- Preheat the oven to 350° F.
- Combine dry ingredients in a large bowl. In smaller bowl, beat the egg and add honey, safflower or canola oil, and applesauce. Mix together and add to dry ingredients. Mix thoroughly into a loose dough. Drop by scant teaspoonful onto a baking sheet covered with greased or non-stick foil. Flatten with the bottom of a glass or jelly jar, if you'd like. Bake for 8 to 10 minutes or until brown. Store in the refrigerator in an airtight container.

Flea Flee Biscuits

Nutritional yeast is said to have flea-repelling properties. It is also high in B vitamins. Some dogs are sensitive to nutritional yeast, however. If you have an itchy dog, you can just leave the yeast out of the recipe (substitute it with the same amount of flour). Garlic, celery seed, and dill are also purported to repel fleas. This treat certainly isn't a substitute for other flea-control practices, but it can augment them nicely.

2 cups whole wheat flour, plus extra for rolling

$1/4$ cup nutritional yeast

1 teaspoon garlic powder

1 teaspoon celery seed

1 teaspoon dried dill

1 egg

$1/2$ cup chicken broth

- Preheat the oven to 400° F.
- Mix the flour, yeast, and seasonings in a large bowl. In a smaller bowl, beat the egg and add the chicken broth. Mix the liquid and dry ingredients together to form a stiff dough. Roll the dough out to about $1/2$-inch thickness on a lightly floured surface and cut into shapes with cookie cutters. Place cookies on a baking sheet covered with greased or non-stick foil and bake for 20 to 25 minutes, or until the tops start to brown. Store at room temperature in a loosely covered container.

Chicken Performance Cookies

This protein- and fat-rich biscuit would be a good one to bring along on an excursion with your dog (like a hike). If you'd like, you can substitute ³/₄ cup of Simple Liver Puree for the baby food.

2 cups whole wheat flour, plus extra for rolling

¹/₂ cup rye flour

1 teaspoon baking powder

¹/₂ teaspoon garlic powder

For the egg wash:

1 egg

Pinch of salt

1 egg

¹/₂ cup safflower oil

2 tablespoons chicken broth

2 (2.5-ounce) jars of chicken baby food

- Preheat the oven to 375° F.
- Combine the flours, baking powder, and garlic powder in a large bowl. In a smaller bowl, beat one egg. Add oil, broth, and baby food to the egg and blend together. Add this mixture to the dry ingredients and mix with a spoon, then knead to incorporate all the dry ingredients. The dough will be soft and somewhat oily. Turn out onto a lightly floured surface and roll out to ¹/₄-inch thickness. Cut into shapes with cookie cutters and place on a baking sheet covered with greased or non-stick foil. Beat the other egg and add a pinch of salt. Brush a little of the egg-and-salt mixture on top of each cookie, to make an attractive glaze. Bake for 15 to 20 minutes or until the tops brown. Store in the refrigerator in an airtight container.

Meaty Kong Stuffers

Hollow Kong toys filled with treats and sealed with something sticky are a great way to occupy a busy dog. These little treats are tasty and healthy and easy to make. You can simply adjust the size so it's appropriate for your dog's Kong. The more difficult the treat is to get out of the opening, the longer your dog will stay occupied!

2 (2.5-ounce) jars of meat baby food

$1/2$ cup wheat germ or wheat bran

$3/4$ cup non-fat dry milk

- Preheat the oven to 350° F.
- Mix all the ingredients together in a large bowl. Roll pinches of the mixture into balls no greater than $3/4$-inches (smaller if your dog is small and you use a small Kong toy). Place balls onto a baking sheet covered with greased or non-stick foil. Alternatively, put the batter into a pastry bag with a $1/4$-inch tip or a plastic sandwich bag with an eighth of an inch clipped off the corner. Squeeze out into small rounds onto the greased baking sheet. Bake for 8 to 10 minutes or until the bottoms are brown. After the treats have cooled, fill a Kong toy with them and seal the hole with cream cheese or peanut butter. Store in the refrigerator in an airtight container.

Liquid Liver Kong Filler

You can pour this fluid mixture into your dog's hollow Kong toy, plug the hole with something thicker, and freeze it. Or put some small treats in it first, then pour in the Kong filler to fill up the empty spaces. Use your imagination in filling your Kong. Just think of this recipe as the glue that holds everything together.

1 pound (2 cups) chicken livers

16 ounces plain yogurt

- Put the chicken livers in a saucepan and cover with water. Bring to a boil and simmer until cooked, about two or three minutes.
- Drain the livers and put in food processor. Add yogurt and blend until smooth.
- Plug the small hole in the Kong with a dab of cream cheese. Put some treats in the Kong, fill it up with the Liver Kong Filler, and then plug the big hole with cream cheese. Freeze for several hours and present it to your happy dog. This should keep your dog busy for quite a while!
- If you like, you can spoon the liver/yogurt mixture into an ice cube tray or paper cups and freeze for several hours for a refreshing snack on a hot day.

Liver Kong Bars

These dense brownie-like bars make great Kong stuffers when cut into the appropriate size. They're so firm that they also cut really nicely into tiny training treats. Chicken livers seem to work a little better than beef liver in this recipe.

$1^1/_4$ cups Simple Liver Puree made from one pound (2 cups) raw chicken livers (see page 112)

$^1/_2$ cup whole wheat flour

$^1/_4$ cup non-fat dry milk

1 egg, beaten

Grated Parmesan cheese

- Preheat the oven to 350° F. Grease the bottom and sides of an 8 x 8-inch pan.
- Make the Simple Liver Puree (with chicken livers). Turn it out into a large bowl and add the flour, dry milk, and egg. Stir to form a thick, sticky batter. Spoon the batter into the pan and push it to the edges. Sprinkle Parmesan cheese on top. Bake for 30 minutes or until firm on top. When cool, cut into narrow bars (or tiny training treats). Store in the refrigerator in an airtight container.

Simple Liver Puree

This recipe isn't for a treat, per se, but for a key ingredient in many treats. It's a delicious one at that! One pound of raw liver makes about 1¹/₄ cups of puree.

Beef or chicken liver (any quantity you like)

- For beef liver: Broil beef liver for about 8 minutes or until top looks cooked and bubbly. Turn over and broil other side for about 4 minutes until bubbly. Don't overcook; if you do the puree will be dry and crumbly, rather than smooth.
- For chicken liver: Place chicken livers, juices and all, into a saucepan. Cover with water and bring to a boil. Then turn down the heat and simmer for about 3 to 4 minutes, until just cooked. Drain.
- For either type of liver, place the cooked liver in a food processor and puree until smooth. Store extra in the refrigerator or freeze for later use.

This thick puree has a multitude of uses:

- Substitute for baby food in recipes that call for meat baby food
- Mix with an equal part of water (or use full strength) and freeze in ice cube trays for a tasty treat on a hot day
- Mix with cream cheese and a little olive oil (to make it spreadable) and use as filling in sandwich treats or frosting for cakes, muffins, or cupcakes
- Coat pills with it to make them a tasty treat
- Add a small amount to dog food to entice your dog to eat
- Seal the end of a stuffed Kong toy

Ingredient Information

Buy the healthiest ingredients that you can afford. Even though these treats are for dogs, who tend to be less than discerning eaters, it's important to pay attention to ingredients. If organic flours, meats, and other ingredients are available to you (and you can make room for them in your budget), spring for the good stuff. Dogs, just like humans, are what they eat. You're being a responsible caregiver when you don't compromise on their food or treats.

Dry Ingredients

Many of the dried ingredients used in this book's recipes are some type of flour. While most people are familiar with all-purpose or white wheat flour, there is a wide variety of other flours available. Most of these alternatives are more nutritious than all-purpose flour. Here is a summary of some of the flours and other dry ingredients included in this book.

All-purpose flour: This flour, which does not include the bran or the germ of the wheat, is easy to work with, rises well, but is among the least nutritious flours listed here. When buying all-purpose flour, you have the choice between bleached and unbleached. Go for the unbleached. Bleaching, which simply makes the already white flour even whiter, eliminates nutrients and flavor, along with the color.

Amaranth flour: This ancient grain has a mild, sweet, nutty flavor. Since it's a fairly obscure flour, your dog has most likely not been exposed to it and therefore should not have a sensitivity to it. This whole-grain flour is gluten free.

Barley flour: This flour is high in fiber and relatively low in protein. It has a nutlike flavor.

Corn meal: This grain, which comes in both yellow and white varieties, adds a nice texture and flavor to recipes. Because many dogs are sensitive to corn, it is included in only a few recipes in this book. If your dog isn't sensitive to it, however, you can substitute it for small amounts of flour or bran.

Flax seed meal: Flax seeds are high in nutritious Omega-3 fatty acids. Flax seed meal is high in fiber and adds a hearty, nutty flavor. Flax seed meal should be stored in the refrigerator.

Garbanzo bean flour: Made from ground chickpeas, this flour is especially good for making grain-free treats. When substituting it for wheat flour, use $^7/_8$ cup of garbanzo bean flour for every cup of wheat flour. It is relatively high in protein.

Oat bran: A good source of fiber, oat bran adds a nice texture to treats.

Oatmeal: These oat flakes, familiar as breakfast cereal, add a rustic texture to treats. In recipes that call for oats, you can use either the old-fashioned rolled oats, with larger flakes, or the smaller, quick-cooking oats. Avoid instant oatmeal, which is pre-cooked.

Quinoa flour: Another ancient grain (like amaranth), quinoa (pronounced KEEN-wa) flour is a good source of fiber and contains all eight essential amino acids. It's gluten free.

Rice flour: Available in white and brown varieties, this flour is appropriate for wheat-sensitive dogs. Brown rice flour, which contains the whole grain (germ, oil, and fiber), is more nutritious, but less easily digested than white rice flour.

Rye flour: This low-gluten flour adds moistness and density to a treat. Dark rye flour contains the germ, oil, and fiber of the rye grass.

Soy flour: Made from roasted, hulled soybeans, this non-grain flour is high in protein and fat. Low-fat soy flour, in which the oil is extracted from the soybeans before grinding, is also available. It is a good source of fiber, vitamins, and minerals and also offers the potentially cancer-protective isoflavones of soy.

Tapioca flour: Made from the root of the cassava plant, this starchy non-grain flour has a gelatinous quality and is very palatable to most dogs.

Wheat germ: Taken from the heart of the wheatberry, wheat germ is high in fiber and protein and has a nutty flavor. Because of its high fat content, it should be stored in the refrigerator or freezer.

Wheat bran: The outer layers of the wheat kernel, wheat bran is high in fiber and, along with the wheat germ, contains most of the vitamins and minerals of the kernel. It adds fiber and texture to the treat.

White bean flour: This non-grain flour is high in protein and fiber. It is made from finely ground white beans (also known as navy beans). It is high in iron, magnesium, and phosphorous and is low in fat.

Whole wheat flour: Unlike all-purpose flour, whole wheat flour contains the germ and the bran of the wheat. It is therefore more nutritious and provides the base of many of the recipes in this book. A white whole wheat flour is also available, which is lighter in color and milder tasting. Whole wheat flour creates a stiffer dough than all-purpose flour.

Wet Ingredients

Liquid ingredients are essential to creating dough. While some provide extra flavor, others add texture or leavening. Oils in this book's recipes are interchangeable. Never use oil that's gone rancid.

Applesauce: Applesauce not only provides flavor, it is a good substitute for oil in low-fat recipes. Use natural applesauce, which doesn't contain added sugar.

Canola oil: A good source of Omega-6 fatty acids, canola oil is another good choice for baking dog treats.

Eggs: Eggs not only hold dough together nicely, they provide leavening, protein, and fat. The recipes in this book were tested using large eggs. If you have another size egg in your refrigerator, give it a try, since the recipes are very flexible. If you want to halve a recipe that calls for one egg, beat the egg slightly and use about $1\frac{1}{2}$ tablespoons of the beaten egg. If you're trying to make a recipe lower in fat, substitute two egg whites for one whole egg.

Honey: Some dogs have a sweet tooth and really enjoy sweet treats. Honey is a healthier sweetener than refined sugar. A tip: If your recipe calls for oil and honey, combine them in the same measuring cup. The oil will keep the honey from sticking to the cup.

Milk: In addition to providing liquid, milk provides flavor that most dogs love. If your dog is sensitive to milk, substitute water. The recipes in this book were created using 2% milk.

Molasses: Another healthy sweetener, molasses has a strong taste and makes a treat quite dark. Blackstrap molasses, which is the waste product of the sugar-making process, is less sweet than other molasses, has more minerals, and is a great way to boost the nutritional value of a recipe that calls for sweetener. If your dog has a delicate palate, he or she may prefer light (the least processed) or dark molasses or, alternatively, honey.

Olive oil: The extra-virgin version of this healthful oil is processed without the use of chemicals, making it a nice, natural ingredient. While its flavor may not necessarily attract dogs, it is typically used in small enough quantities that this isn't an issue.

Safflower and sunflower oil: These oils are good sources of Omega-6 fatty acids, which are important to dogs' health. They're flavorless and an excellent choice in baking for dogs. Look for cold- or expeller-pressed oils, which don't use chemicals in processing.

Flavorings

In addition to dry and wet ingredients, each recipe has some sort of flavoring that makes it appetizing to a dog. Here are just a few of the flavorings used in this book.

Baby food with meat: Pureed meat from the baby food aisle is an easy-to-use and delicious ingredient in dog treats. Compared with other meat ingredients, like liver, it is expensive, however. Look for meat-and-broth baby food (like "chicken and broth" or "turkey and broth") rather than meat-and-gravy baby food because the latter typically contains cornstarch. That is a problem if your dog is sensitive to corn. You can also use meat-and-vegetable baby food, but it might not pack the flavor punch of meat alone.

 **Fish:** Canned salmon or tuna makes a great flavoring for treats. Other types of canned fish work too. Buy the tuna packed in water, not oil, so you don't end up with more oil than the recipe needs. Because tuna contains mercury, be sparing in feeding your dog tuna treats. Canned salmon comes in several grades. You can buy the least-expensive grade, which usually includes skin and even bone. Your dog should be able to digest these without difficulty.

Fresh garlic: Dogs enjoy the taste of garlic, and it's purported to have flea-repelling properties. You can buy pre-minced garlic that you keep in your refrigerator, if you don't want to chop or crush garlic for recipes.

You can also substitute ⅛ of a teaspoon of garlic powder for a clove of fresh garlic. Since my dog, Pip, can't tolerate garlic (it gives her digestive difficulties), garlic is used relatively sparingly in this book. Feel free to add this flavoring (or any flavoring) if the recipe doesn't call for it.

Garlic powder: Because it's in powdered form, garlic powder tends to be easier to use than fresh garlic. You can substitute garlic powder for fresh garlic if you prefer. Be sure to use garlic powder, not garlic salt, since your dog doesn't need the added salt.

Non-fat dry milk: Non-fat dry milk isn't the most natural ingredient in the world, but it's very tasty to dogs. Sprinkle non-fat dry milk on top of any biscuit dough to add a tasty, crunchy topping. Look for organic non-fat dry milk as a healthier alternative.

Liver: Dogs love liver. It's a frequently used ingredient in the recipes of this book, simply because it's nutritious and most dogs are so motivated by it. You can use beef or chicken livers pretty much interchangeably in the recipes. You can also use turkey liver, pork liver, or any other livers you can find. If you can find and afford it, use organic liver whenever possible, since the liver is the organ that processes toxins.

Peanut Butter: Most dogs love peanut butter. Use natural peanut butter, which isn't loaded with sugars and chemicals. I use freshly ground peanut butter from the health food store (they have a machine so you can grind it yourself), which contains nothing but peanuts.

Sources:

Bittman, Mark. *How to Cook Everything*. Hoboken: Wiley, 1998.

Rombauer, Irma S. and Marion Rombauer Becker. *Joy of Cooking*. New York: Plume, 1973.

Bob's Red Mill labels: www.bobsredmill.com

www.wholehealthmd.com

www.epicurious.com

www.nutritiondata.com

Sources for Ingredients

If your neighborhood grocery store doesn't have the ingredients you're looking for, try a health- or natural-food store. In many cities, large chain natural food stores, like Whole Foods and Wild Oats, carry virtually anything you need. If you've never been in one, you might be amazed at what they have to offer.

Asian markets can also be a great source for unusual flours or meat sources. For example, you can often find pork liver at an Asian market, which can be great if your dog has a beef or chicken allergy, or just nice for variety in your liver treats. You can also find dried, shaved fish flakes, called bonito fish flakes, which can be sprinkled on top of treat dough before baking. (If you have a cat, share the bonito flakes!)

If you don't have a local access to unusual flours, you can buy them online from Bob's Red Mill, a premier maker of whole-grain flours. Visit them at www.bobsredmill.com.

Some purveyors of frozen raw-food diets sell ingredients that can be used in treats. For example, fresh ground salmon works very well in salmon treats. In addition, you can buy whole turkey hearts or other organs for grinding, as well as pre-ground liver mixed with other organs. If your dog is allergic to more common protein sources, like chicken, turkey, and beef, you can purchase other, more exotic meats from these companies with which you can make treats. For example, ostrich, kangaroo, buffalo, and venison are all available. If you're going to be baking treats with these meats, be sure to buy boneless ground meat. Raw-food companies include Oma's Pride (www.omaspride.com) and Bravo (www.bravorawdiet.com).

For More Information

Cancer Diets

Veterinary oncology expert Greg Ogilvie, DVM, has performed extensive research on cancer and diets. He notes his findings in his article "Nutrition and Cancer: Frontiers for Cure!" For dogs with cancer, Dr. Ogilvie recommends fewer simple carbohydrates. This article can be found online at:

http://web.archive.org/web/20010213234901/http://www.cvmbs.colostate.edu/cancercure/nutrition.htm

Home-Prepared Diets

Billinghurst, Ian. *The BARF Diet: Raw Feeding for Cats and Dogs Using Evolutionary Principles*. Lithgow, N.S.W.: Ian Billinghurst, 2001.

—*Give Your Dog A Bone*. Lithgow, N.S.W.: Ian Billinghurst, 1993.

—*Grow Your Pup with Bones*. Lithgow, N.S.W.: Ian Billinghurst, 1998.

Lonsdale, Tom. *Raw Meaty Bones Promote Health*. South Windsor, N.S.W.: Revetco P/L, 2001.

Morgan, Diane. *Feeding Your Dog for Life: The Real Facts About Proper Nutrition*. Sun City, Ariz: Doral Publishing, 1992.

Schultze, Kymythy. *Natural Nutrition for Dogs and Cats: The Ultimate Diet.* Carlsbad, Calif.: Hay House, 1998.

Segal, Monica. *K9Kitchen: Your Dogs' Diet: The Truth Behind the Hype.* Toronto: Doggie Diner, Inc., 2002.

Strombeck, Donald. *Home-Prepared Dog and Cat Diets: The Healthful Alternative.* Ames, Iowa.: Iowa State University Press, 1999.

Volhard, Wendy and Kerry L. Brown. *Holistic Guide for a Healthy Dog. 2d ed.* Foster City, Calif.: Howell Book House/IDG Books Worldwide, 2000.

Natural Health Care For Pets

Allegretti, Jan and Katy Sommers, D.V.M. *The Complete Holistic Dog Book: Home Health Care for Our Canine Companions.* Berkeley, Calif.: Celestial Arts, 2003.

Flaim, Denise. *The Holistic Dog Book: Canine Care for the 21st Century.* New York: Howell Book House, 2003.

Goldstein, Martin. *The Nature of Animal Healing: The Definitive Holistic Medicine Guide for Caring for Your Dog and Cat.* New York: Ballantine Books, 1999.

Hamilton, Don. *Homeopathic Care for Dogs and Cats: Small Doses for Small Animals.* Berkeley, Calif: North Atlantic Books, 1999.

Pitcairn, Richard and Susan Hubble Pitcairn. *Dr. Pitcairn's Complete Guide to Natural Health for Dogs and*

Cats. 2d ed. Emmaus, Pa.: Rodale Press, 1995.

Puotinen, C.J. *The Encyclopedia of Natural Pet Care*. New Canaan, Conn.: Keats Publishing, 1998.

Wulff-Tilford, Mary L. and Gregory L. Tilford. *All You Ever Wanted to Know About Herbs for Pets*. Irvine, Calif.: Bowtie Press, 1999.

Training and Activities

Alexander, Melissa. *Click for Joy! Questions and Answers from Clicker Trainers and Their Dogs*. Waltham, Mass.: Sunshine Books, 2002.

Coile, D. Caroline, Ph.D. *Beyond Fetch: Fun, Interactive Activities for You and Your Dog*. New York: Howell Book House, 2003.

Miller, Pat. *Positive Perspectives: Love Your Dog, Train Your Dog*. Wenatchee, Wash.: Dogwise Publishing, 2004.
—*The Power of Positive Dog Training*. New York: Howell Book House, 2001.

Pryor, Karen. *Getting Started: Clicker Training for Dogs*. Waltham, Mass.: Sunshine Books, 2001.

Tillman, Peggy. *Clicking with Your Dog: Step-by-Step in Pictures*. Waltham, Mass.: Sunshine Books, 2001.

Sources for Great Dog Stuff

For most, if not all, of the aforementioned books:

www.dogwise.com

www.sitstay.com

For bait bags:

www.sitstay.com

www.doggonegood.com

For dog-themed Chinese take-out container gift boxes:

www.doggonegood.com

For great specials on toys:

www.petedge.com

For the "My Dog Can Do That!" board game:

www.doglogic.com/books2.htm

For info on Kong products and recipes for Kong stuffing:

www.kongcompany.com

For info on Kong Time, the Kong-dispensing machine in development:

www.proactivepet.com

APPENDIX FOUR

For Our International Audience– Conversion Tables

Generic Formulas for Metric Conversion

Ounces to grams	multiply ounces by 28.35
Pounds to grams	multiply pounds by 453.5
Cups to liters	multiply cups by .24
Fahrenheit to Centigrade	subtract 32 from Fahrenheit, multiply by five and divide by 9

Oven Temperatures

Degrees in Fahrenheit	Degrees in Centigrade	British Gas Marks
200°	93.0°	—
250°	120.0°	—
275°	140.0°	1
300°	150.0°	2
325°	165.0°	3
350°	175.0°	4
375°	190.0°	5
400°	200.0°	6
450°	230.0°	8

Metric Equivalents for Volume

U.S.	Imperial	Metric
⅛ tsp	—	.6 ml
½ tsp.	—	2.5 ml
¾ tsp.	—	4.0 ml
1 tsp.	—	5.0 ml.
1½ tsp.	—	7.0 ml
2 tsp.	—	10.0 ml.
3 tsp.	—	15.0 ml
4 tsp.	—	20.0 ml
1 Tbsp.	—	15.0 ml
1½ Tbsp.	—	22.0 ml
2 Tbsp. (⅛ cup)	1 fl. oz	30.0 ml
2½ Tbsp.	—	37.0 ml
3 Tbsp.	—	44.0 ml
⅓ cup	—	57.0 ml
4 Tbsp. (¼ cup)	2 fl. oz	59.0 ml
5 Tbsp	—	74.0 ml
6 Tbsp.	—	89.0 ml
8 Tbsp. (½ cup)	4 fl. oz	120.0 ml
¾ cup	6 fl. oz	178.0 ml
1 cup	—	237.0 ml (.24 liters)
1½ cups	—	354.0 ml
1¾ cups	—	414.0 ml
2 cups (1 pint)	16 fl. oz	473.0 ml
4 cups (1 quart)	32 fl. oz	(.95 liters)
5 cups	—	(1.183 liters)
16 cups	128 fl. oz	(3.8 liters)

Metric Equivalents for Weight		Metric Equivalents for Length (use also for pan sizes)	
U.S.	**Metric**	**U.S.**	**Metric**
1 oz	28 g	¼ inch	65 cm
2 oz	58 g	½ inch	1.25 cm
3 oz	85 g	1 inch	2.50 cm
4 oz (¼ lb.)	113 g	2 inches	5.00 cm
5 oz	142 g	3 inches	6.00 cm
6 oz	170 g	4 inches	8.00 cm
7 oz	199 g	5 inches	11.00 cm
8 oz (½ lb.)	227 g	6 inches	15.00 cm
10 oz	284 g	7 inches	18.00 cm
12 oz (¾ lb.)	340 g	8 inches	20.00 cm
14 oz	397 g	9 inches	23.00 cm
16 oz (1 lb.)	454 g	12 inches	30.50 cm
		15 inches	38.00 cm

Metric Equivalents for Butter	
U.S.	**Metric**
2 tsp.	10.0 g
1 Tbsp.	15.0 g
1½ Tbsp	22.5 g
2 Tbsp. (1 oz)	55.0 g
3 Tbsp.	70.0 g
¼ lb. (1 stick)	110.0 g
½ lb. (2 sticks)	220.0 g

INDEX